AF522129

हिंदी-अंग्रेजी

मुहावरा-लोकोक्ति कोश

हिंदी–अंग्रेजी

मुहावरा-लोकोक्ति कोश

कैलाशचंद्र भाटिया

प्रकाशक • **प्रभात प्रकाशन प्रा. लि.**
4/19 आसफ अली रोड,
नई दिल्ली–110002

संस्करण • 2025
मूल्य • आठ सौ रुपए
मुद्रक • नरुला प्रिंटर्स, दिल्ली

HINDI-ANGREZI MUHAWARA-LOKOKTI KOSH
(Hindi-English Dictionary of Idoms & Proverbs)
by Dr. Kailash Chandra Bhatia ₹ 800.00
Published by Prabhat Prakashan Pvt. Ltd., 4/19 Asaf Ali Road, New Delhi-2
e-mail: prabhatbooks@gmail.com ISBN 978-93-5266-275-3

अपनी बात

भावों और विचारों की अभिव्यक्ति सुस्पष्ट, सशक्त एवं प्रभावपूर्ण बनाने हेतु भाषा में मुहावरों तथा लोकोक्तियों का विशेष महत्त्व है। मुहावरा भाषा का वह विशिष्ट गुण है जिससे भावाभिव्यक्ति चमत्कृत हो उठती है। जब किसी शब्द-समूह का सामान्य अर्थ न लेकर उससे मिलता-जुलता सांकेतिक-लाक्षणिक अर्थ लिया जाता है तब उसे मुहावरा कहा जाता है, जैसे 'नाक कट गई' में कोई यह देखने लगे कि नाक तो ठीक-ठाक है, कहीं से कटी नहीं तो वह नासमझी होगी।

मुहावरे में प्रधान है उसका लाक्षणिक अर्थ जिसका गठन अपरिवर्तनीय रहता है। गठन में परिवर्तन होते ही उसका लाक्षणिक अर्थ बेमजा हो जाता है। 'कमर टूटना' को न 'कटि भंग' कर सकते हैं, न 'कटि टूटना'। मुहावरे अधिकतर शारीरिक अंगों व चेष्टाओं, सामाजिक-राजनैतिक कथनों व घटनाओं पर आधारित होते हैं। मुहावरे में क्रियापद रहता है, जैसे—अँगूठा दिखाना, आँख दिखाना, अपना उल्लू सीधा करना आदि। हिंदी के मुहावरे तद्भव शब्दों पर आधारित हैं : हस्त, अक्षि, कर्ण, नासिका के स्थान पर मुहावरों में हाथ, आँख, कान, नाक का ही प्रयोग होगा और यही मुहावरेदानी हिंदी-उर्दू को परस्पर बाँधे हुए है।

लोक में प्रचलित उक्ति ही 'लोकोक्ति' है, जो किसी देश या काल से बँधी नहीं होती। वह तो सार्वकालिक व सार्वदेशिक है। लोकोक्तियाँ मानवीय अनुभवों के आधार पर बनती हैं। लोकोक्ति में संक्षिप्तता, सारगर्भिता, विदग्धता आदि गुण भरपूर होते हैं।

मुहावरे वाक्य का अंश होकर आते हैं जबकि लोकोक्ति/कहावतें

पृथक् से वाक्य का रूप लेते हैं। किसी कथन की पुष्टि करने के लिए सम्यक् लोकोक्ति का प्रयोग कर दिया जाता है। मुहावरों का जब वाक्य में प्रयोग किया जाता है तो उसकी क्रिया में, मात्र क्रियारूप में लिंग, वचन के अनुसार परिवर्तन हो जाता है, अन्य अंश में नहीं, जैसे—'फूलकर कुप्पा हो जाना' पुल्लिग-स्त्रीलिंग में समान रहेगा; स्त्री के संबंध में कहने पर 'फूलकर कुप्पी' होना कदापि नहीं होगा।

मुहावरों-लोकोक्तियों का अक्षरश: अनुवाद दूसरी भाषा में नहीं किया जा सकता, यह मालूम होते हुए भी यह लघु प्रयास है, जिसमें समानांतर भावभूमि को दूसरी भाषा—अंग्रेजी—में प्रस्तुत किया गया है। इस दिशा में परमप्रिय डॉ. तुमनसिंह की लघु कृति प्रकाशित हुई। हिंदी-अंग्रेजी कोशों में मूल शब्द के साथ कुछ मुहावरे और प्रयोग भी दिए जाने लगे। इस दृष्टि से डॉ. तिवारी व डॉ. कपूर के कोशों के अतिरिक्त मैं दो शब्द-कोशों के नामों का उल्लेख करना चाहता हूँ, जिनकी सहायता ली गई—(छैलबिहारी मिश्र) 'अभिनव हिंदी-अँगरेजी-हिंदी कोश', आलोक भारती, 1991; (आर.एस. मैक्ग्रैगर) 'हिंदी-इंग्लिश डिक्शनरी', 'आक्सफर्ड', 1995।

ऐसे कोशों में पूर्णता का दावा करना उचित नहीं। भाषा में निरंतर वृद्धि होती रहती है। देखते-देखते पिछले कुछ माह में 'हवाला' से संबंधित शब्दावली और उसकी अर्थच्छटाएँ कहाँ-से-कहाँ पहुँच गईं।

इस कोश में मुहावरों/लोकोक्तियों के अलग-अलग अर्थों को वर्णक्रमानुसार क्रम संख्या द्वारा तथा समानार्थकों को अर्धविराम द्वारा दर्शाया गया है। प्रयोगकर्ताओं के सुझावों का स्वागत किया जाएगा।

लोक सभा सचिवालय के सेवा-निवृत्त वरिष्ठ संपादक श्री ओम प्रकाश काश्यप ने कोश के वर्तमान स्वरूप में प्रकाशन में भरपूर सहयोग दिया जिसके लिए मैं उनका हृदय से आभारी हूँ।

—कैलाशचंद्र भाटिया

मुहावरे

अंक भरना / लगाना	To embrace
अंक में लेना	To take one in the lap, To enfold
अंकुर जमना	Germination of seeds
अंकुर जमाना	To plant out sprouts
अंकुश में रखना	To hold in submission, To keep in check
अंकुश लगाना	To goad
अंकुश होना	To have control over
अंग छूकर कहना	To swear devotion to
अंग फूले न समाना	To be in a rapture
अंग लगना	1. To be assimilated 2. To be embraced 3. To nourish the body (food)
अंगद का पाँव	Irrevocably firm
अंगारा बनना / होना	To be wild with rage, To flush with rage
अंगारे उगलना	1. To be fierce and fiery in speech 2. To spew venom 3. To utter venomous words

अंगारे बरसना	To be excessively hot (esp temperature during the ho season)
अंगारों पर पैर रखना	To jump into hot waters
अंगारों पर लोटना	To burn with rage, envy
अँगूठा दिखाना	To refuse point blank, To gesture with the thumb ir defiance
अँगूठे पर मारना	To regard as contemptible
अंगूर खट्टे होना	Grapes are sour, To decry what is inaccessible, To speak slightingly of things that are beyond one's reach
अंजर-पंजर ढीले होना	1. To be out of order (appliance) 2. To become tired and fagged out (body)
अंजर-पंजर तोड़ना	To give severe beating
अंजलि देना	To pay homage/tribute
अंजलि-भर	Handful
अंजाम देना	To carry out a task
अंटसंट बकना	To talk nonsense, To advance rambling arguments
अंटी देना / मारना	To hide something (between the fingers), To pilfer
अंत पा लेना	To fathom the secret
अंत भला सो भला	All is well that ends well

अंतिम यात्रा (महायात्रा)	One's journey's end, Death
अंतिम साँस लेना	To breathe one's last
अंदर करना	To put behind the bars, To put inside
अंदाज लगाना	To make an estimate, To conjecture, To evaluate
अंधा करना	To deceive, To render incapable to perceive the reality
अंधा बनना	To feign blindness
अंधी गली के मुहाने पर	To be at a dead end
अंधी सरकार	Indiscreet administration, An apathetic government
अंधे की लकड़ी / लाठी	Helpless man's only assistance
अंधे के हाथ बटेर लगना / लग जाना	1. A prize kill by a blind man 2. To have an unexpected gain 3. To have a windfall 4. To hit the mark
अंधे को अंधा राह दिखाए	When the blind lead the blind, both shall fall into the ditch
अंधे को सब हरा-ही-हरा दिखाई देता है, सावन में	Everything looks yellow to a jaundiced eye
अंधेर मचाना	To commit an outrage, To unleash a reign of terror, To oppress
अँधेरी रात, चार दिन की चाँदनी फिर	A nine day's wonder

अँधेरे घर का उजाला	1. A light in darkness 2. The only son
अँधेरे-मुँह (मुँह)	Wee hours of the morning
अँधेरे में तीर चलाना	(To try) to hit in the dark, To strike without taking an aim
अँधेरे में रखना	To keep in dark
अंधों में काना राजा	A figure among cyphers, Triton among the minnows
अकेला पड़ना	To be left alone
अकेला-दुकेला	Alone or with one a two more
अकेली जान	All alone
अक्ल का आदमी, उलटी	A man with brain topsy-turvy, Addle-headed
अक्ल का अंधा	(Person) devoid of commonsense, Bereft of brains
अक्ल का दुश्मन (मूर्ख)	A stupid person, Dunderhead
अक्ल काम न करना	To be at a loss, To be in a fix
अक्ल के घोड़े दौड़ाना	1. To cudgel one's brains 2. To indulge in mental gymnastics
अक्ल के पीछे लट्ठ लिये फिरना	1. To be pursuing a course of folly 2. To act in a grossly foolish way
अक्ल चकराना	To be non-plussed/confused

अक्ल चरने जाना (घास)	1. Have the wits gone a wool-gathering 2. To be at one's wit's end 3. To take leave of one's senses 4. To lose power of discrimination
अक्ल ठिकाने न रहना	Wits lost their moorings
अक्ल ठिकाने लगाना / ठीक करना	To set (one) right, To cut to size
अक्ल दंग रह जाना	To be dumb-founded
अक्ल पर पत्थर पड़ना	1. To be confused 2. To be out of one's wits 3. To be dumb-founded 4. To take leave of one's senses
अक्ल पर परदा पड़ना	To be confused, to have lost one's wits
अक्ल भिड़ाना/लड़ाना	To exercise one's intellect, To rack one's brains
अक्ल मारी जाना	To lose one's wits
अखाड़ा जमना	The muster was on, To assemble animatedly
अखाड़े में आना / उतरना	To step into an arena
अखाड़े में उतरना	To accept challenge, To pick up the gauntlet
अगर-मगर करना	1. Dilly-dallying 2. Resorting to ifs and buts/ irrelevant arguments 3. Wavering 4. Yea and nay

अचार डालना	Oh! the folly of keeping so much
अच्छा बोओ अच्छा काटो	He who sows well reaps well
अच्छी कटना	To be well, To have good time
अच्छे आना	To reach (unexpectedly) at a right moment
अच्छे-अच्छों से पाला पड़ना	To have tussles with toppers
अटकल-पच्चू (पच्ची) —अनुमान करना	1. At random 2. Fictitious (मनगढ़ंत) 3. Mere conjecture 4. Rough estimate
अटकल लगाना	Guess, speculation, conjecture
अटकल से	At random, By guess/conjecture
अड़ंगे पर चढ़ाना	To bring into a vulnerable position, To gain an advantage over
अड्डा जमाना	To stick to a place unusually long
अड्डा बनाना	To turn a place into an off-time resort
अता-पता नहीं (कुछ)	No clue, No whereabouts
अता-पता मिलना	To reach a clue
अथ से इति तक	From beginning to end
अदा करना	1. To accomplish (a task) 2. To discharge 3. To pay debt 4. To perform in due manner

अदा करना, पार्ट	To play the role
अदा करना, फर्ज	To do one's duty
अदा करना, रस्म	To observe a ceremony/ritual
अदा करना, शुक्रिया	To give thanks
अधर में झूलना/लटकना	To hang in the balance, To remain in suspense
अधर में पड़ना	To remain in doubt
अधिकार जताना	To assert one's rights, To lay a claim
अधिकार जमाना	1. To come into possession 2. To establish control over
अनंतकाल तक	Till eternity
अनंत, हरि, हरिकथा अनंता	Infinite is the Lord and infinite are his glories
अनबन होना	To be at loggerheads with
अनाप-शनाप खर्च	Indiscriminate/reckless expenditure
अनाप-शनाप बकना	To babble, To talk loose
अन्न-जल उठ जाना (दानापानी उठना)	1. To be forced to move away from a particular place 2. To be obliged to leave 3. End of means of sustenance at a particular place
अन्न-जल छोड़ना	To give up food and water (To fast)
अपना-अपना, पराया-पराया	Blood is thicker than water, The tie of kindred is real
अपना उल्लू सीधा करना	To have an axe to grind,

	To serve one's own ends (by befooling others)
अपना क्या जाता है?	What do we lose?
अपना बोझ आप उठाना	To paddle one's own canoe
अपना भला-बुरा पहचानना	To know on which side one's bread is buttered,
	To know wherein lies one's good and bad
अपना-सा मुँह लेकर रह जाना	To cut a sorry figure,
	To hang one's lip in humiliation
अपना-सा मुँह लेकर लौट आना	To return with disappointment writ large on one's face
अपना हाथ जगन्नाथ	Depend on none but yourself,
	If you want a thing well done, do it yourself
अपनी-अपनी पड़ना	To be concerned with one's own affairs,
	To think in terms of one's own interests
अपनी कब्र खुद खोदना	To dig one's own grave,
	To do anything that would tend to harm one's own interests,
	To drive a nail into one's own coffin
अपनी नाक कटवाना	To disgrace oneself,
	To spoil one's own good name
अपनी नींद सोना	To be free of care,
	To sleep like a log
अपने दोष न देखे, दूसरे के गिने	The pot calls the kettle black

अपने पाँव पर आप कुल्हाड़ी मारना	To act against one's own interests, To adopt suicidal policy, To harm oneself by acting foolishly
अपने मुँह मियाँ मिट्ठू बनना	To indulge in self-praise, Self-praise is no recommendation
अपमान सहना	To pocket an insult
अफवाह उड़ाना / फैलाना	1. To defame 2. To spread rumours
अब-तब करना	To evade by delaying tactics, To put off
अब-तब की लगी रहना / होना	To be at death's door
अबे-तबे करना	To talk rudely, To address disrespectfully
अरण्य रोदन करना	1. Cry in wilderness 2. Unacknowledged advocate of some reform
अरमान ठंडे पड़ना	Hopes having dashed to the ground
अरमान निकलना	To be satiated
अरमान निकालना/पूरा करना	1. To gratify one's long-cherished desire 2. To have it off
अरमान रह जाना	Not to have one's aspirations materialised
अर्थ (अरथ) का न होना, किसी	To be good for nothing
अर्थ लोभ अनर्थ की जड़	Lure of money is the root cause of all evils

अलग-थलग करना	1. To be isolated 2. To be quarantined 3. To leave high and dry
अल्लाह को प्यारा हो जाना	To kick the bucket
अवसर पर न चूकना	Strike the iron while it is hot
अशर्फियाँ लुटें और कोयलों पर मुहर	Pennywise, pound foolish, Spare at the spigot and spill at the bung

आँख अटकना	To fall in love with
आँख आना	To have sore eyes
आँख उठाकर देखना	To look someone in the eye
आँख उठाना	To cast a hostile look
आँख ओझल, पहाड़ ओझल	Out of sight, out of mind
आँख का अंधा	A dimwit, A nitwit
आँख का अंधा गाँठ का पूरा	A nitwit with a fat purse
आँख का काँटा	An eye sore
आँख का काजल चुराना	1. To be a very expert thief 2. To steal with great dexterity
आँख का तारा	Apple of one's eyes, Darling
आँख का पानी उतर जाना/मर जाना	Not to blush at all, To become shameless, To lose honour
आँख खुल जाना	1. To be aroused from sleep 2. To come back to earth 3. To stop being impractical
आँख खुलना	To be disillusioned,

	To be put on the alert
आँख गड़ाना	To gaze, To stare
आँख गरम करना	To feast one's eyes with the sight of something appealing
आँख चढ़ना	1. To be drowsy from intoxication 2. To flash with anger 3. To have the eyes upturned
आँख चुराना	1. To avoid being noticed 2. To avoid catching one's eye 3. To disregard 4. To look the other way
आँख चूकना	Supervision to relax, To let the opportunity slip by
आँख छिपाना	To avoid being sighted, To be timid
आँख झपकना	1. To feel sleepy 2. To take/have a nap
आँख टेढ़ी करना	To cast a wrathful look, To look angry
आँख ठंडी होना	To be pleased
आँख डबडबाना	To have the eyes moist with tears
आँख डालना	To look with eyes amorous
आँख तरेरना	To look angrily To look daggers at someone
आँख निकालना	1. To cast a wrathful glance

	2. To threaten
आँख पथराना	To be stunned beyond words
आँख पलटना	To turn supine, To withdraw favour or regard suddenly
आँख पसारना	To be ready to welcome with an open heart
आँख फटना	1. To be consumed with envy 2. To be utterly astonished
आँख फूटना	To be jealous, to feel dislike
आँख फूटी पीर गई	Relief gained at too high a price
आँख फैलाना	To look aghast
आँख भरकर देखना	To cast affectionate or amorous looks to one's satisfaction
आँख मारना	To shut one eye briefly to signal an amorous intention or connivance
आँख मिचना	To pass away, to die
आँख लगना	1. To fall in love 2. To have a doze
आँख लड़ना	1. To exchange amorous glances 2. To fall in love
आँख लाल करना	To glare furiously
आँख सेंकना	To feast one's eyes with things of beauty
आँख से उतरना / गिरना	To fall from grace
आँख से दूर, दिल से दूर	Out of sight, out of mind
आँखें खुल जाना	To serve as an eye opener
आँखें खुली की खुली रह जाना	To be all but stunned

आँखें खोलना	To enlighten
आँखें गरम करना	To feast one's eyes
आँखें तरसना	To long for (to see or meet somebody)
आँखें दिखाना	1. To adopt a threatening posture, to cast a threatening look 2. To defy openly 3. To look angry 4. To show hostility
आँखें निकालना	To look very angry, To show temper
आँखें नीची होना	To be humiliated
आँखें फाड़-फाड़कर देखना	To cast a bewildered look, To stare at with bewildered eagerness
आँखें फेरना	To turn one's attention away from, To withdraw one's affection/ favour
आँखें बंद करना	1. To die 2. To ignore 3. To neglect
आँखें बचाना	1. To avoid being noticed 2. To slink away
आँखें बदल लेना	To change one's stance
आँखें बिछाना	1. To be ready to accord warmest welcome 2. To wait most eagerly

आँखें भर आना	To be in tears
आँखें भर लाना	To be on the verge of crying
आँखें मुँदना	To die, to pass away
आँखें मूँदकर रखना	Blindly, thoughtlessly, To keep one's eyes shut
आँखें रखना	1. To attend 2. To look at 3. To stare (admiration)
आँखें रोशन करना	To be joyful
आँखें लाल-पीली / नीली-पीली होना	To be beside oneself with anger
आँखों के बल (क्रि. वि.)	1. Carefully 2. Willingly
आँखों देखा हाल	Running commentary
आँखों न सुहाना (फूटी)	To hate the very sight of
आँखों पर पट्टी बाँधना	To be blind to a reality
आँखों पर परदा पड़ना	1. Not to see the obvious 2. Not to see the writing on the wall 3. To be under an illusion
आँखों पर बिठाना	To accord a hearty welcome, To treat with great honour
आँखों में खून उतरना	In a state of great anger, Up the wall
आँखों में गढ़ना / चुभना	1. To arouse unpleasant feelings 2. Hard on the eyes
आँखों में चढ़ना	To be held in esteem, To think much of someone

आँखों में धूल झोंकना / डालना	1. To cheat 2. To deceive, to trick one 3. To mislead someone by misrepresentation 4. To pull wool over a person's eyes 5. To throw dust in the eyes of someone
आँखों में बसना / समाना	To be ever present in one's mind's eye
आँखों में रात काटना	To keep awake the whole night
आँखों से परदा हटना	To be disenchanted
आँच आना	1. To come to harm 2. To suffer
आँच क्या, साँच को	Truth fears none What has truth to fear from the fire?
आँच खाना	To be heated, To become angry
आँच न आना	No harm to come
आँचल बिछाना	To receive with warm hospitality
आँचल में बाँधना	1. To bear in mind 2. To etch in one's memory 3. To keep one under one's complete control
आँतें गले आना / पड़ना	1. To be in a desperate strait 2. To be in distress
आँतें गले समेटना	To go without food

आँतें गले सूखना	To be awfully hungry
आँधी की तरह आना	To come suddenly like a storm
आँधी के आम	A windfall, Things obtained easily, Unexpected gain
आँय-बाँय बकना	To beat about the bush
आँसू, आठ-आठ (रोना)	To cry one's heart out, To weep bitterly
आँसू पी जाना	To conceal one's grief, To suppress one's tears
आँसू पोंछना	To console, To wipe away the tears
आँसू बहाना	To shed tears
आँसू भर लाना	To begin to weep
आ कूदना	To barge in, To burst into
आ टपकना	To drop in
आ निकलना	To turn up
आ पड़ना	1. To attack 2. To befall (misfortune etc.)
आ बनना	To afflict (one)
आ बैल मुझे मार	To ask for trouble, To invite attack
आ लगना	To come (in time)
आईना दिखाना	To show (a person) what he is
आईना देखना	To weigh one's capabilities
आईने में मुँह देखना, पहले	First deserve, then desire
आकाश कुसुम	An impossibility
आकाश के कुलाबे मिलाना	Conditions to become favourable

आकाश के तारे तोड़ लाना	1. To perform a miracle
	2. To square the circle
आकाश छूना	To be sky high
आकाश पर दिया जलाना	To show overweening conceit
आकाश पाताल एक करना	To move heaven and earth
आकाश बाँधना	1. To achieve the impossible
	2. To talk conceitedly
आकाशबेल जैसा होना	Living the life of a parasite,
	To go on the bum
आकाश से गिरा खजूर पर अटका	Out of the frying pan into the fire
आकाश से बातें करना	To be as lofty as sky
आग पर पानी डालना	To calm down, to pacify
आग पर लोटना	1. To be burning with jealousy
	2. To be on pins and needles
आग फूँकना	To stir up a quarrel
आग-फूस का बैर	Innate hostility
आग-बबूला होना	To be enraged,
	To flare up,
	Wild with rage
आग बरसना	Extremely hot,
	Scorching/sweltering heat
आग बुझाना	1. To satisfy hunger
	2. To pacify a quarrel
आग भड़कना	To be stirred,
	To flare up (as emotions)
आग में घी डालना	1. To add fuel to the fire
	2. To aggravate passion
	3. To pour oil on the flames

आग में पानी डालना	To pacify matters
आग में हाथ डालना	To expose oneself to danger needlessly, To place one's hand in lion's mouth, To take the bear by the tooth
आग लगना	To be a victim of green-eyed god
आग लगने पर कुआँ खोदना	To lock the stable after the steed is stolen
आग लगाकर तमाशा देखना	To join the spectators after causing a fire-break, To witness a brawl engineered by oneself
आग लगाकर पानी को दौड़ाना	To make a show of remedying a dire situation created by oneself
आग लगाना	1. To destroy completely 2. To foment trouble 3. To play mischief 4. To set on fire 5. To sow seeds of dissension
आग सुलगाना	To kindle fire, To incite/stir up strife
आग हो जाना	To be wild with rage
आगा-पीछा करना	To hesitate, To vacillate
आगा-पीछा देखना	To consider beforehand all conceivable aspects of a matter

आगा-पीछा सोचना	To weigh pros and cons
आगे आना	1. To come forward 2. To come in the forefront 3. To come to light
आगे करना	To place at the front, To promote
आगे की राम जाने	God alone knows what is in store
आगे कुआँ पीछे खाई	Between the devil and the deep sea, Between Scylla and Charybdis, On the horns of a dilemma
आगे देखना	To act prudently or carefully
आगे पीछे कोई न होना	To have no kith or kin
आगे बढ़ना	1. To excel, to surpass 2. To make headway
आज-कल करना	To evade, to postpone, to put off
आज-कल लगना	To be on death bed
आजाद करना	To be set free
आजाद रहना	To live independently
आजाद होना	To be independent
आजिज आना / रहना	To be helpless
आटा गीला करना	To make one's life miserable
आटा गीला होना, गरीबी में	A pimple has grown upon an ulcer
आटे में नमक	In small proportions
आटे में नमक बराबर	Like a drop in the ocean
आटे-दाल का भाव मालूम होना	1. To be faced with stark realities of life

	2. To know how strange are the ways of the world
आठ-अठारह होना	1. To be confused, to be distressed 2. To be scattered
आठ-आठ आँसू रोना	1. To cry one's heart out 2. To shed flood of tears
आठों गाँठ कुम्मैत	1. Very clever, every inch a crook 2. Very cunning 3. Most skillful
आठों पहर	Day and night, Day in and day out, Round the clock
आड़ देना	To provide shelter to
आड़ में आना	To conceal oneself
आड़ लेना	To take shelter
आड़े आ जाना / पड़ना	To serve as an impediment
आड़े आना	1. To come between 2. To come in the way of
आड़े समय	1. Against a rainy day 2. At the time of difficulty 3. During difficult times 4. In adversity
आड़े-हाथों लेना	1. To give a bit of one's mind 2. To rebuke, to chide 3. To take to task
आड़े होना	To become crooked
आता-जाता नहीं	To know nothing

आत्मा ठंडी होना	A longing to be fulfilled
आत्मा मसोसना	1. To subdue one's emotional upsurge 2. To suffer distress 3. To suppress one's desire
आत्मा सताना	To inflict grief/pain/sorrow/suffering
आदमी बनना	To learn good manners/etiquettes
आदमी बनाना	1. To educate 2. To teach good manners/etiquettes
आदमी होना	1. To become civilised 2. To become a worthy human being
आदी होना	To be addicted to/to get used to/habitual
आधा तीतर, आधा बटेर	Neither fish nor fowl
आधी बात कहना	To hold something back
आधे पेट	Half starved
आन मानना	To yield to
आन उतरना	1. To become dull 2. To be disgraced
आन रखना	To keep a vow
आनन-फानन में (अविलंब)	1. Forthwith 2. Instantaneously 3. Without delay
आना-जाना होना	On visiting terms
आने, सोलहों	Completely

आनाकानी करना	1. To evade, to hesitate 2. To make excuses 3. To procrastinate
आप-आप करना	To flatter
आप काज महाकाज	Do it rather than get it done, One's own achievement beats the rest, Self done well done
आप बीती	One's own first hand experience
आप बुरा जग बुरा	Evil mind, evil find, One who is giddy thinks the world turning round
आप भला तो जग भला	Good mind, good find
आप मरे जग परलो (प्रलय)	After me, the deluge (I care not what happens when I am dead) The death's day is the doom's day
आप सुखी जहान सुखी	If you are happy, the whole world is happy, Self is the first consideration
आपकी सीख आपको मुबारक	Keep your sermons to yourself, To save your breath to cool your porridge
आपा खोना	1. To lose one's individuality 2. To sacrifice one's self
आपा-धापी पड़ना	1. To enter into a stiff competition

	2. To struggle for one's self-interest
आपे में आना	To become sober, To return to the normal state
आपे से बाहर होना (अपने से)	1. To become impatient 2. To drive (one) to distraction 3. To lose one's composure, to lose one's temper
आफत उठाना	To create havoc, To suffer distress/misfortune
आफत का परकाला	A dare devil
आफ़त की पुड़िया	Bundle of trouble
आफत ढाना / मचाना	1. To make undue haste 2. To unleash troubles/sufferings
आफत मोल लेना/सिर पर लाना	1. To bring misfortune upon oneself needlessly 2. To invite trouble
आबरू खाक में मिलाना	To bring dishonour on oneself
आबरू पर पानी फेरना	To fall into disgrace
आबरू में बट्टा लगाना	1. Stain upon one's honour 2. To tarnish one's honour
आबरू लूटना	To outrage one's modesty, To violate one's chastity
आम के आम गुठलियों के दाम	1. Earth's joys and heaven's blessings combined 2. Money for money and interest besides 3. To kill two birds with one stone

आम[१] खाने से मतलब पेड़ गिनने से नहीं	1. Gather in the harvest, why count the stalks 2. To be concerned with the substance rather than the source
आम[२] तौर पर (साधारणतया)	Generally, usually
आम फहम	1. Language of the common man 2. Popular (a work)
आरसी क्या, हाथ कंगन को	A self-evident fact requires no proof
आरी चलाना (कलेजे पर)	To feel pangs of jealousy
आरी चलाना (गरदन पर)	To do incalculable harm
आवश्यकता आविष्कार की जननी है	Necessity is the mother of invention
आवाज उठाना	To raise voice in protest, to spread a report
आवाज कसना	To have a fling at, To pass unsavoury remarks against, To speak out against
आवाज पड़ना, कानों में	To hear randomly
आवाज पर लगना	To obey a call
आवाज भर्राना	1. Voice choked with emotion 2. Voice to turn husky
आशा टूटना	Hope to be shattered, To lose hope
आशा निराशा में गोते लगाना	To hang between hope and despair
आशा बाँधना (बहु. आशाएँ)	To cherish a hope,

	To entertain hopes
आशाओं पर पानी फेरना	To throw cold water on one's hopes and ambitions
आस टूटना	No hope
आसन उखड़ना	To be dislodged, to be shaken
आसन छोड़ना	To leave seat, To relinquish office/position
आसन जमना	To be seated firmly
आसन जमाना	To be glued to one's seat
आसन डिगना/डोलना	To feel insecure/shaky (in office), To get panicky/nervous, Throne/seat to wobble
आसन देना	To offer seat
आसन मारना	To stick to a place/position
आसन लगना	To take a posture
आसन लगाना	To sit obstinately until one's demands are satisfied
आसन हिलना	To be in an unsteady position
आसमान के तारे तोड़ना	To achieve the impossible
आसमान छूना (कीमतें)	To rise sky-high
आसमान जमीन के कुलाबे मिलाना	To boast wildly
आसमान टूटना	To be overtaken by misfortune
आसमान टूट पड़ना	1. Heavens to fall 2. To be struck by a calamity
आसमान पर उड़ना	To roam in the realm of unreality, To be vainglorious
आसमान पर चढ़ाना	To praise to the skies, To spoil by extravagant praise/flattery

आसमान पर थूकना	To puff against the wind, To try to humiliate the really great
आसमान पर होना (दिमाग)	To be too big for one's boots
आसमान में छेद करना	To attempt the impossible
आसमान में छेद होना	To rain incessantly
आसमान में थिगली लगाना	To be too crafty
आसमान सिर पर उठा लेना	To create a ballyhoo, To raise hullabaloo
आसमान से गिरना	1. To drop down too low 2. To get (something) from unknown quarters 3. A godsend
आसमान से गिरा खजूर में अटका	Out of frying pan into the fire
आसमान से बातें करना	To skyrocket, To touch the skies, to be lofty
आस्तीन का साँप	A foe in the garb of a friend, A snake in the grass
आस्तीन चढ़ाना	1. To be prepared for a fight 2. To gird up one's loins
आस्तीन में साँप पालना	To treat ungrateful persons with kindness
आह पड़ना	To be afflicted by a curse, To be under a curse, To suffer the consequences of wrong-doing
आह लेना	To be cursed for wrong-doing, To provoke the curse of
आहट लेना	To try to get a clue of

इक्कीस होना	To go one better, To have the pull over person
इज्जत उतारना / खोना	To put to disgrace
इज्जत के पीछे पड़ना	To be intent on ruining one's honour
इज्जत डुबोना	To ruin one's reputation
इज्जत, दो कौड़ी की (कर देना)	To lose one's honour, To heap disgrace
इज्जत पर पानी फेरना	To bring the name of one's family into disrepute, To have one's reputation sullied
इज्जत पर हाथ डालना	To try to violate the modesty (of a woman)
इज्जत बिगड़ना	To lose respect
इज्जत मिट्टी में मिलाना	Honour comes to dust
इज्जत में बट्टा लगना	To have one's reputation sullied
इज्जत लूटना	1. To disgrace 2. To outrage the modesty (of a woman) 3. To ravish

इज्जत लेना	1. To insult 2. To treat with dishonour 3. To violate (a woman)
इतना-सा मुँह निकलना	1. His countenance fell, 2. His face fell, 3. To look aghast
इतना सा मुँह रह जाना	To feel small
इतनी-सी बात होना	Too trifle a matter
इधर-उधर की हाँकना	1. To beat about the bush 2. To talk tall, to talk boastfully
इधर-उधर होना	To be in a state of disorder, To be in disarray
इधर का उधर होना	To turn topsyturvy
इधर की उधर करना / लगाना	1. To indulge in backbiting 2. To carry tales 3. To misrepresent
इधर कुआँ उधर खाई	Between the devil and the deep sea, On the horns of a dilemma
इधर-उधर में रहना	To waste time in idle pursuits
इलायची बाँटना	To invite to a marriage ceremony
इल्लत लगाना	To acquire a bad habit, To get addicted to
इशारा, आँख का	To wink
इशारे पर चलना/नाचना	To dance to the tune of
इशारों पर नचाना	To make one dance to the tune of
इस हाथ दे, उस हाथ ले	As you sow, so shall you reap, Early sow, early mow

ईंट का जवाब ईंट / पत्थर से देना	To give as good as one gets, To pay in the same coin, To retort adequately in words or deeds, Tit far tat
ईंट-से-ईंट बजाना	1. To bring to ruination 2. To cause strife 3. To shatter the defences to pieces
ईद का चाँद होना	To be seen once in a blue moon, Visits to become few and far between, To make a rare appearance
ईमान की कहना	To speak the truth
ईमान बेचना	To break one's word To sell one's conscience to
ईश्वर के दरबार में देर है, अंधेर नहीं	God's mill grinds slow but sure

उ

उँगली उठना	To be an object of ridicule
उँगली उठाना	To censure, To defame
उँगली दबाना, दाँतों तले	To be stunned to the core, To be wonderstruck
उँगली दिखाना	1. To find fault with 2. To threaten
उँगली पकड़कर पहुँचा पकड़ना	Give him an inch and he would take an ell, Give him a little licence and he will take great liberties
उँगलियाँ (पाँचों) घी में होना	1. To be in the most advantageous position 2. To have gains galore 3. To have one's bread buttered on both sides 4. To wallow in luxury
उँगलियाँ देना, कानों में	To turn a deaf ear
उँगलियों पर नचाना	To make one dance to one's tune,

	To twist around one's little finger
उँगलियों पर नाचना	To act in deference to someone's desires, To dance to the tune of
उखड़ जाना	To ruin, To be uprooted
उखड़ना (पैर)	To lose firmness, To lose hold
उखड़ना (रंग)	To lose charm
उखड़ी-उखड़ी बातें करना	To talk drily
उखाड़ना, गड़े मुर्दे	To dig up things buried deep, To rake up old wounds
उगलना, आग	To eject fire
उगलना, जहर	To spew venom
उगाना, हथेली पर सरसों	To attempt the impossible
उछल-कूद मचाना	To do a lot of capering
उछालना, नाम	To disgrace one's name
उछालना, पगड़ी	1. To insult publicly 2. To treat (one) disrespectfully
उजला मुँह होना	Honour to be restored
उजागर करना	To bring on the surface, To bring to the fore
उठा न रखना, कोई बात/कोर-कसर	To leave no stone unturned
उठ बैठना	To recover
उठाना, जोखिम	To take risk
उठाना, प्रश्न	To raise a question
उठाना, बीड़ा	To pick up the gauntlet, To undertake a responsibility with a pledge

उड़ती खबर	Hearsay, rumour Unconfirmed report
उड़ती चिड़िया पहचानना	1. To know the rook as it is seen 2. To know which way the cat jumps 3. To spot the puck in the crowd
उड़ना, हवा	Air is rife
उड़ना, हवाइयाँ (चेहरे पर)	1. All the glow of one's face is gone 2. To be at one's wit's end
उड़ान भरना/ मारना, कल्पना की	1. To build castles in the air 2. To make flights of imagination
उड़ाना, धज्जियाँ	To reduce to shreds
उड़ाना, बेपर की	To brag about, To talk tall
उड़ाना, हँसी में	To laugh away
उड़ा ले जाना	To carry away/off, To kidnap
उतरना, चित्त से / निगाह से	1. To be forgotten 2. To fall from grace 3. To fall in one's eyes
उतरना, चेहरा	To be dejected, To be downcast, To be gloomy
उतरना, हाथों की मेहँदी	Wedding to be just over
उतावला सो बावला	Haste makes waste, Hurry spoils curry

उत्साह ठंडा कर देना	To dampen the spirits, To throw cold water on one's enthusiasm
उथल-पुथल करना	To make a commotion
उथल-पुथल मचाना	To cause a turmoil/an upheaval, To go on a rampage
उदर भरना	To feed oneself, To support oneself
उधार खाए बैठना	1. To be intent on something 2. To become one's mortal enemy
उधार प्यार की कैंची है	Lend and lose a friend
उधेड़-बुन में पड़ना	1. To be in a fix 2. To be on the horns of a dilemma
उन्नीस-बीस होना	To be slightly better or worse, To be almost equal
उफ न करना	To endure without complaint
उफ न निकलना	Not to let out even a sigh, To bear silently
उबल पड़ना	To be infuriated
उबलना, क्रोध से	To be beside onself with rage
उबलना, खून	To make one's blood boil, To be enraged
उबाल ठंडा होना	To cool down
उबाल निकालना, मन का	To give vent to one's feelings, To vent one's spleen
उभार लाना	To protrude or project, To induce

उमड़ना-घुमड़ना	1. To gather (thick clouds) 2. To gather thoughts, to be emotional 3. To be moved
उमड़ना, मन	To be full of emotion, To thrill (heart)
उम्मीदों पर पानी फेरना	Hopes to be shattered, To throw cold water on one's hopes
उलझन खड़ी करना	To create complication
उलझन में डालना	To complicate matters, To put one in a dilemma
उलझन में पड़ना	To be in a quandary, To be involved in a tangle
उलटकर कहना	To retort, To quip
उलट पड़ना	1. To return 2. To turn over, to assail
उलट-पुलट करना	To overturn, To turn upside down
उलट-बँसी-बाँसी	A suggestive paradox throwing light
उलटा चोर कोतवाल को डाँटे	The thief threatens the police
उलटा-पलटा (तितर-बितर, अस्त-व्यस्त)	Confused, topsy-turvy, To be at sixes and sevens
उलटा हाथ जमाना	To deal a backhander, To strike someone a backhanded blow
उलटी खोपड़ी	Blockhead, pervert, wrong-headed

उलटी पट्टी पढ़ाना	To misguide, To poison the mind of
उलटी माला फेरना	To invoke a curse upon
उलटी सीधी सुनाना	To give someone a piece of one's mind
उलटी हवा बहना	1. Blowing of ill wind 2. Things moving in the wrong direction 3. To have a run of bad luck
उलटे छुरे / उस्तरे से मूँड़ना	To fleece, To rob someone of his money by befooling
उलटे पाँव लौटना / फिरना	To return forthwith, To return without wasting time
उलटे मुँह गिरना	To fall into a trap laid for another
उल्टी गंगा बहाना	1. To carry coals to Newcastle 2. To do things the wrong way 3. To go against traditions 4. To put the cart before the horse
उल्लू, काठ का	Blockhead, duffer, dullard
उल्लू फँसाना	To entrap a green-horn, To make a fool of
उल्लू बनाना	1. To befool 2. To cheat, to deceive 3. To expose oneself to ridicule 4. To make an ass of 5. To pull someone's leg

उल्लू बोलना	A desolate place
उल्लू सीधा करना	To have one's own axe to grind, To serve one's own ends

ऊँच-नीच समझना	To consider or know all conceivable aspects of a matter
ऊँचा चढ़ना	To rise to eminence
ऊँचा-नीचा दिखाना	To blow hot and cold to deceive
ऊँचा बोल	Tall talk
ऊँचा हाथ रहना	To dominate, to excel
ऊँची-नीची सुनाना	To give a dressing down
ऊँचे-नीचे पाँव पड़ना	To err, To falter, To go astray, To stumble
ऊँचे बोल का मुँह नीचा	Pride hath a fall
ऊँट किस करवट बैठता है ?	1. Let us see which way the cat jumps 2. Let us see which way the wind blows
ऊँट की चोरी और नीचे-नीचे	To try to conceal what is conspicuous

ऊँट बदनाम, शहर में	Give a dog bad name and hang him
ऊखल / ओखली में सिर देना	To invite trouble wilfully, to invite disaster
ऊपर का दम भरना	To pretend affection, or regard.
ऊपर लेना, अपने	To take upon oneself

ए

एक अकेला दो ग्यारह	Union is strength
एक अनार सौ बीमार	1. One post, a hundred candidates 2. There are always more round pegs than round holes
एक आँख न भाना	To be allergic to, To have absolutely no liking for
एक आँख से देखना	To look impartially on, To treat all alike
एक एक कौड़ी दाँत से पकड़ना	To be stingy to a penny
एक ओर कुआँ, एक ओर खाई	Between the devil and the deep sea
एक की चार लगाना	To exaggerate beyond measure
एक गंदी मछली सारे तालाब को गंदा कर देती है	One dirty fish spoils the whole pond
एक चने से भाड़ नहीं फूटता	1. A lone soldier cannot win a battle 2. A single misfortune will not bring disaster

	3. One man cannot manage the whole show single-handed
एक दो दिन मेहमान, तीसरे दिन—	Fish and visitors smell in three days
एक न चलना	1. All efforts to come to naught 2. Not to succeed
एक नजीर सौ नसीहत	An example is better than precept
एक पंथ दो काज	To kill two birds with one stone
एक परहेज सौ इलाज	Prevention is better than cure
एक फूल से माला नहीं बनती	One flower makes no garland
एक म्यान में दो तलवारें नहीं समातीं	Two of a trade seldom agree
एक लाठी से हाँकना	To paint everyone with the same brush, To treat all alike
एक से इक्कीस होना	To progress by leaps and bounds
एक-से-बढ़कर एक	One on top of the other
एक से दो भले	Two heads are better than one
एक ही थैली के चट्टे-बट्टे	Chips of the same block, Cast in the same mould
एक ही रट लगाना/राग अलापना	To harp on the same tune/on one string
एक होना	1. To be unique 2. To be united
एक हाथ से ताली नहीं बजती	It takes two to make a quarrel
एकादशी मनाना	To have nothing to eat, to starve

एड़ियाँ घिसना	To make herculean efforts
एड़ियाँ रगड़ना	1. To be in great deal of trouble for long 2. To die by inches
एकै साधे सब सधैं सब साधै सब जाए	A rolling stone gathers no moss
एड़ी चोटी का जोर लगाना	1. To move heaven and earth 2. To put in all possible efforts 3. With might and main
एड़ी चोटी का पसीना एक करना	1. To exert one's best endeavours 2. To spare no efforts
एड़ी से चोटी तक	1. From head to heel 2. From top to bottom 3. From top to toe

ऐंच तानकर ठीक करना	1. To bring one round to one's views by hook or by crook 2. To straighten out twists and turns
ऐंठ दिखाना	To show off conceit
ऐंठन न गई, रस्सी जल गई	To be full of airs, though vanquished
ऐंड़ी-बेंड़ी सुनाना	1. To call names 2. To give one a piece of one's mind
ऐरा-गैरा नत्थू खैरा	1. Every Tom, Dick and Harry 2. Tag-rag and bobtail
ऐसी-तैसी	Damn it, Let it go to hell
ऐसी-तैसी करना	To make a mockery, To revile, To teach one a lesson

ओखली में सिर देना / डालना	To undertake a challenging task, To invite trouble deliberately
आँख ओझल, पहाड़ ओझल	Out of sight, out of mind
ओट, परदे की (में)	Secretly, clandestinely
ओढ़ना	To take upon oneself (blame or responsibility)
ओढ़ना, दोष	To be the scapegoat
ओर देखना, अपनी	To see to one's own interests
ओले गिरना, सिर मुँड़ाते ही (ओले पड़ना / गिरना / बरसना)	1. Misfortune to overtake at the very outset 2. Occurrence of a mishap at the very start
ओस चाटे प्यास नहीं बुझती	1. Dew drops cannot quench one's thirst 2. Fog cannot be dispelled by a fan
ओहदे का रोब छाँटना	To pull one's rank on

औंधा बखत (वक्त)	1. Evil fortune 2. Hard times
औंधी खोपड़ी	Block-head, Perverted
औंधे मुँह गिरना	To be badly deceived, To be badly misled, To be ruined
औकात पहचानकर चलना	1. To be conscious of one's inferior position/rank in life and act accordingly 2. To know one's place
औकात बसर करना	To pass (one's) days
औकात से बाहर होना	To cross one's limits, To go beyond one's capacity
औने-पौने करना	To haggle
औने-पौने दामों पर निकालना	To dispose of something below par
औने-पौने बेचना	To dispose of at throw-away prices

कंगन तो आरसी क्या, हाथ	The obvious needs no proof
कंगाली में आटा गीला	A pimple has grown upon an ulcer
कंधा डालना / डाल देना	1. To give up attempt in despair 2. To lose heart
कंधा देना	To lend a shoulder in carrying a dead body, To take a corpse on its bier
कंधे से कंधा मिलाकर चलना / भिड़ाना	To stand shoulder to shoulder, To work hand in hand
कंधे से छिलना	A dense crowd
कंधे से लगाना	To lay (a child) against one's shoulder
कंधे पर लेना (अपने)	To shoulder responsibility
कंधों पर उठाना	To accord a rousing welcome
कंबख्ती का मारा	Afflicted by ill luck
कंबल डालकर	Surreptitiously
कंबल पर रंग चढ़ाना, काले	To attempt the impossible, to waste one's time

कई धंधों में हाथ होना	To have too many irons in the fire
ककड़ी-खीरा समझना	To treat others as far inferior to oneself
कच-कच करना	To chatter, to prattle
कचूमर निकलना	To be at one's wits' end
कचूमर निकालना	1. To reduce someone to a pulp 2. To render unserviceable by misuse
कच्चा, कान का	One who readily believes everything, Too credulous
कच्चा चिट्ठा खोल देना	1. To disclose the dark side of someone's life 2. To recite misdoings of 3. To reveal the inside story
कच्चा, जी (करना)	To feel disheartened/heart-broken To lose heart
कच्चा-पक्का करना	To leave incomplete, to spoil
कच्चा-पक्का संदेशा	Unauthentic message
कच्चा-पड़ना	1. To be hamstrung, 2. To lose face
कच्ची गोटी/गोली खेलना	1. To act in an immature way 2. To be a green-horn
कच्ची-पक्की सुनाना	To call names
कच्ची बात	Loose talk
कटकर चला जाना	To avoid, To turn away from

कटघरे में खड़ा होना	To be put in the dock
कटा-कटा रहना	To maintain distance, To avoid coming face to face
कटी पतंग की तरह होना	To be in a desperate state, To fall like a log
कटे पर नमक छिड़कना	To add insult to the injury, To make matters worse
कठपुतली, हाथों की	Puppet in the hands of (some one)
कड़वा घूँट पीना	1. If you don't like it, you may lump it 2. To submit to the disagreeable
कड़वा दिल करना	To bear without complaint
कड़वा हो जाना	To become bitter
कड़ाई करना	1. To be austere 2. To be strict
कड़ाका गुजरना	1. To fast long 2. To suffer a hard time
कड़ा दिल करके देना	To give grudgingly
कड़ा दिल करके सुनना	To listen with a heavy heart
कड़ी-कड़ी सुनाना	To give a bit of one's mind, To speak harshly
कड़ी निगाह रखना	To keep a close watch
कढ़ाही में हाथ डालना	To submit to an ordeal
कढ़ी, बासी (में उबाल आना)	1. To become surcharged with emotion despite declining years 2. Momentary excitement

कतर-ब्योंत करना	1. To make deductions 2. To plan 3. To prune
कतराना, कतराकर निकल जाना	To avoid being noticed and walk away
कथनी करनी में अंतर	Difference between promise and performance, Difference between saying and doing
कथनी से करनी भली	Example is better than precept, It is better to do well than to say well
कदम उखड़ना	To lose ground
कदम उठाना	To take action, To take steps
कदम गाड़ना	To get a foothold, To secure one's footing
कदम दिखाना	To make tracks
कदम बढ़ाना	To move ahead, To progress
कदम रखना	1. To enter 2. To follow 3. To venture (upon)
कन्नी काटना	To avoid, To fight shy of
कन्नी-दबना	To be in a tight spot
कन्नी-मारना	To lean to one side
कपड़े उतार लेना	To disrobe, To fleece

कपड़े रँगना	To become ascetic, To renounce the world
कपाल खुलना	Fortune to take a favourable turn
कपाल फूटना	Misfortune to befall, To be unfortunate
कफन फाड़कर उठना	To appear suddenly from nowhere
कफन बाँधकर निकलना	1. To burn one's boats 2. To cut off all of one's ways to retreat 3. To set out on a hazardous journey or undertake a risky job, unmindful of the dangers involved
कफन सिर से बाँधना	1. To be ready to face death 2. To engage in a risky enterprise 3. To risk life
कबर/कब्र के मुरदे उखाड़ना	To rake up old issues
कबर/कब्र खोदना	To adopt means to ruin, To dig grave
कबर/कब्र में पैर रखना/होना	1. To be very old 2. To be on the point of death 3. To have one foot in the grave
कभी धूप-कभी छाँव	Pleasures and pains are closely woven in the web of life
कभी-न-कभी	At some time or the other, Seldom, sooner or later
कमर कसना/बाँधना	1. To brace oneself up

	2. To get ready for
	3. To gird up (one's) loins
	4. To screw up one's courage
कमर टूटना	To do back-breaking work,
	To lose self-confidence
कमर तोड़ना	1. To break the back of
	2. To deal a severe blow
	3. To discourage
कमर थामना	1. To encourage
	2. To support (someone)
कमर सीधी करना	To relax for a while
कमाए कोई, खाए कोई	One beats the bush, another has the hare,
	To feed oneself on the earnings of others
कमान खींचना/चढ़ाना	To enjoy supremacy
कमाल करना	To perform a miracle,
	To set the Thames on fire,
	To take one's breath away
कमाल दिखाना	To work wonders
कमाल रखना	To be perfect,
	To have mastery over
कर गुजरना	To carry through
करत-करत अभ्यास के जड़मति होत सुजान	Practice makes a man perfect
कर देखना	To test/try
करधनी टूटना	1. To grow poor
	2. To grow weak
	3. To lose heart

करनी खाक की, बात लाख की	Much smoke, little fire, Great boast, small roast
करम ठोकना	1. To bewail one's fate 2. To lament over one's lot
करम फूटना	1. To fall on evil days 2. To have a stroke of ill luck
करवट बदलना	1. To take a new turn 2. To turn to new interests/ friends
करवट लेना	To turn over
करवटें बदलना	To be restless
करवटों में काटना	To be on pins and needles, To pass time restlessly
करेला नीम चढ़ा	An unpleasant situation getting worse
कल का आदमी	1. An upstart 2. A recent arrival
कल के छोकरे	Babes and sucklings
कल किसने देखा है	No one has seen tomorrow
कल की बात	1. A recent occurrence 2. A thing of recent past
कल नाम, काल का	Do not put off till tomorrow what you can do today, Tomorrow never comes
कलई खुलना	The real traits (of) to be exposed, To be exposed
कलई खोल देना	To expose, to unmask
कलई खोलना	To unmask the real qualities (usually in bad sense)

कलम उठाना	To take up one's pen,
	To start writing
कलम का धनी होना	To wield a formidable pen
कलम घसीटना	1. To scribble
	2. To write profusely
कलम तोड़ना	To write something wonderful,
	To write par excellence,
	Writing to excess
कलम फेरना	To write off, to cancel
कलम बंद करना	To take down in writing
कलम में जादू होना	To wield a mighty pen
कलम में जोर होना	To wield an effective pen
कली खिलना, दिल की	To be thrilled with joy,
	To feel jubilant
कलेजा उछलना	Heart to leap with joy
कलेजा उड़ा जाना	To be anxious
कलेजा कड़ा करना	To take courage in both hands
कलेजा काँपना	To be afraid
कलेजा काटना	1. To bare one's heart
	2. To be struck with terror
	3. To be terrified
	4. To sacrifice, to do resolutely at great cost
कलेजा खिल उठना	Blossoming of the heart,
	To be beside oneself with joy
कलेजा छलनी होना	Heart pierced like a sieve,
	To prick the heart a great deal
कलेजा जलना	To burn with envy
कलेजा टूक-टूक होना/टूटना	To be disheartened,

	To suffer a deep emotional shock
कलेजा ठंडा करना	To gratify oneself
कलेजा पक जाना	To come to the end of one's tether, To reach limits of endurance
कलेजा, पत्थर का	To steel one's heart
कलेजा बल्लियाँ उछलना	To be on top of the world
कलेजा मलना	To feel frustrated
कलेजा मसोसकर रह जाना	To feel agonising helplessness
कलेजा मुँह को आना	To be grief-stricken, To have one's heart in one's mouth
कलेजा सुलगना	Burning with grief or jealousy
कलेजे का टुकड़ा	1. An apple of one's eyes 2. Closest to one's heart
कलेजे पर आरी चलना	To fall victim to green-eyed god
कलेजे पर साँप लोटना	To be tormented by jealousy
कलेजे पर हाथ रखना	1. To consider objectively 2. To hear the voice of one's conscience
कलेजे से लगाना	1. To cherish 2. To hold someone as one's own
कसक निकालना	To soothe one's hurt feelings by retaliation
कसक मिटाना	To get even with
कसक रह जाना	A burning sensation to continue, Sting to persist

कसना पड़ेगा	To be brought under control, To be tightened
कसम उतारना	To carry out an obligation nominally, To set free of the bonds of oath
कसम खाने को	Nominally, To meet an obligation in short supply
कसर उठा न रखना	To leave no avenue unexplored, To leave no stone unturned, To spare no efforts
कसर छोड़ना	To leave much to be desired, To leave scope for doing certain things
कसर निकालना	1. To make good the loss 2. To make up deficiency 3. To retaliate 4. To settle old scores
कसर रह जाना	1. To be wanting in one thing or the other 2. To fall short
कसाई के खूँटे से बँधना	To be handed over to a brute, To get wedded to a merciless man
कसौटी पर कसना	1. To test, to prove 2. Actual testing
कसौटी पर खरा उतरना	To prove oneself equal to the task, To stand a test

कहना कुछ, करना कुछ	Double dealing, Professing one thing and doing another
कहना-सुनना (समझाना)	To explain, to persuade
कहना-सुनना (झगड़ना)	To dispute, to wrangle
कहर टूटना	1. A bolt from the blue 2. A calamity to befall
कहर ढाना/तोड़ना	1. To bewitch (by her beauty) 2. To cause a devastation 3. To create havoc
कहानी, राम	1. A lengthy account (लंबा-चौड़ा वृत्तांत) 2. A tale of woe 3. One's life story
कहीं-का-कहीं	1. At the wrong place 2. A square peg in a round hole
कहीं-का-कहीं पहुँचना	To make great strides
कहीं का न छोड़ना	To be driven to the dogs
कहीं का न रहना	To be completely undone
कहीं पहुँचना	To attain great heights
काँटा, रास्ते का	Obstacle in the way
काँटा हो जाना, सूखकर	To be reduced to a skeleton
काँटा होना	1. To act as an obstacle 2. To be an eye-sore
काँटे की तरह खटकते रहना	Constant source of annoyance, To be an eye-sore
काँटे की लड़ाई	Very keen contest, bitter struggle
काँटे बिछाना, रास्ते में	To create difficulties in one's way

काँटे बोना	1. To sow seeds of distress or misfortune 2. To sow troubles
काँटे से काँटा निकाला जाता है	One nail drives another
काँटों का ताज	1. An authority difficult to wield 2. Crown of thorns 3. Uneasy lies the head that wears the crown
काँटों में घसीटना	1. To drag one into trouble 2. To embarrass by undue praise
काँटों-सा खटकना	To be offensive to the sight
काई की तरह फटना	To get scattered
काई-सा फट जाना	To be dispersed
कागज काला करना	1. To raise loan by filling in necessary papers 2. To waste both paper and ink 3. To write
कागज की नाव	1. A house built on sand 2. A house of cards 3. An insecure scheme
कागज की नाव नहीं चलती	1. Fraud does not prosper 2. Fraudulent means do not pay in life 3. Something which will not survive long
कागजी घोड़े दौड़ाना	To do unnecessary paper work
काज करना	To accomplish a task
काज सँवारना	1. To achieve a goal 2. To fulfil someone's wish

काजल की कोठरी	An affair from which one cannot emerge unscathed
काटना, बात	To interrupt
काटना, समय	To while away time
काटने दौड़ना	1. To fly into a rage 2. To talk aggressively
काटो तो खून नहीं	1. To be in a blue funk 2. To be paralysed by sudden fear
काठ का उल्लू	Consummate idiot
काठ की हाँड़ी	Deception which can be practised only once
काठ मार जाना	To be stunned beyond depth
काठ हो जाना	To be petrified
कान कतरना / काटना	To outwit, To prove more than match
कान का कच्चा	Over-credulous, Ready or inclined to believe
कान खड़े करना / खड़े होना	1. To be alarmed 2. To be alert 3. To prick up one's ears
कान खाना	To nettle, To pester, To rub the wrong way
कान खोलकर सुनना	To lend a careful ear, To listen with all attention
कान दबाए चले आना	To slink away
कान पर जूँ तक न रेंगना	1. To be very negligent 2. To go in one ear and out the other

	3. To pay no heed to
कान फूँकना	To whisper
कान भरना	To poison the ears
कान में उँगली देना	To turn a deaf ear
कान में डाल देना	To apprise someone (of something)
कान में तेल/रुई डालना	1. To be inattentive 2. To refuse to listen
कान में पड़ना	To come to know, To reach one's ears
कान लगाकर सुनना	To be all ears, To listen eagerly
कानी कौड़ी	Something of too small a value
कानी कौड़ी न होना, पल्ले	To be almost penniless
कानून छाँटना	To try to impose one's own interpretations on others
कानों-कान खबर न होना	To guard a secret too closely, To maintain absolute secrecy
कानों-कान कहना	To spread a news by whispering campaign, To whisper
कानों-कान न जानना	Not to divulge a secret
कानों-कान न सुनना	Not letting anyone get a clue
काम अटकना	1. The work is suspended due to some obstruction 2. To depend on somebody
काम, आज का, आज करना	Do not put off till tomorrow what you can do today, Do today's work today and not tomorrow

काम आना	1. To be killed in action 2. To be of help 3. To die in the battlefield 4. To serve a purpose
काम की बात होना	To do something worthwhile
काम को काम सिखाता है	Practice makes a man perfect
काम चलना	To achieve the objective
काम चलाना	1. To improvise 2. To keep the work going 3. To make do with 4. To manage
काम तमाम करना	1. To do away with, to put an end to 2. To finish a task/business 3. To kill
काम निकालना	1. To get work done 2. To achieve one's purpose
काम प्यारा है, चाम नहीं	Handsome is that handsome does
काम रोको (प्रस्ताव)	Adjournment motion
काम लगाना	To get oneself employed
काम-से-काम	To mind one's own business
काम से जाता रहना	1. To be given the sack 2. To be rendered jobless 3. To wash one's hands of one's work
काम होना	1. Life to come to an end 2. To cease to exist
कायम करना	1. To appoint

	2. To establish
	3. To set up
	4. To uphold
कायम रखना	1. To keep up
	2. To preserve
कायम रहना	1. To stand firm
	2. To survive
कायल करना	1. To convince fully
	2. Unable to answer
कायल होना	1. To acknowledge
	2. To be convinced of
काया-पलट करना	1. To change radically
	2. To overhaul
काल का मारा	1. An ill-fated person
	2. Famine-stricken
काल के गाल में समाना	To die, to pass away
काल पाकर	In due course of time
काल बिताना	To while away time
काल, सिर पर (नाचना)	Death to be impending
काला कानून	Black law
काला चोर	1. Master thief
	2. Some mysterious hand
काला, मुँह (करना)	1. To blacken one's face
	2. To demean oneself
	3. To disgrace oneself
कालिख पोतना / लगाना, मुँह पर	1. To put to shame
	2. To tarnish one's image
कालिख लगाना (नाम पर)	1. To earn a bad name
	2. To besmirch one's reputation

काली करतूत	Evil deeds
काली कमलिया / कामरी पर चढ़े न दूजो रंग	Black will take no other hue
काले से सफेद करना	1. To do impossible task 2. To launder black money 3. To paint black as white
काले कोसों	A long way off, far off
काले दिल का	Black-hearted
का वर्षा जब कृषि सुखाने	1. After death, the doctor (Help arrived when it was too late) 2. To lock the stable after the steed is stolen
काशी करवट लेना	To suffer extreme hardship
किंकर्त्तव्यविमूढ़ होना	1. Perplexed 2. To be in a fix, to be in a quandary 3. Uncertain what to do
किनारा करना / काटना	To abstain, to keep away from
किनारा खींचना	To break off, to refrain
किनारे करना	To brush aside, to set aside
किनारे न जाना	To refrain from going nearby
किनारे पहुँचना	To reach the conclusion
किनारे लगना	To reach the destination
किनारे लगाना	To bring to a conclusion
किनारे हो जाना/होना	To dissociate, to step aside
किया कराया	1. Achievements 2. Deeds
किया पाना, अपना	To reap what one has sown

किए पर पछताना	To repent of one's own deeds
किरकिरा करना	To mess up, To spoil
किरकिरा, मजा (हो जाना)	To mar the pleasure of
किराए का आदमी	A hessian, A mercenary
किराए का टट्टू	Hireling
किला जीतना	To come out triumphantly
किला टूटना	Fall of a game
किले बनाना / बाँधना (हवाई)	To build castles in the air
किल्ली गाड़कर बैठना	To become adamant, To be unyielding
किल्ली घुमाना	To turn a control
किल्ली दबाना	To pull strings
किस खेत की मूली (हो) ?	You are not worth a rap
किस गिनती में हो ?	You count for nothing
किस चिड़िया का नाम है ?	1. Does he at all count ? 2. He is of no account
किस मुँह से (कहते हो) ?	What face do you have to say so?
किसान चाहे वर्षा, कुम्हार चाहे सूखा	Donkey means one thing and the driver another
किसी की करनी भरना	To pay for the sins of others
किसी को बैंगन बावले, किसी को पथ्य	One man's meat is another man's poison
किस्मत आजमाना	To try one's luck
किस्मत उलटना	Fortune to take a turn for the worse
किस्मत के खेल	Designs of destiny

किस्मत का चक्कर	Irony of fate
किस्मत का धनी	A lucky guy, Very fortunate person
किस्मत का फेर	A stroke of ill luck
किस्मत का बदा	Ordained by destiny
किस्मत की बात	Matter of fortune
किस्मत खुलना/जागना/पलटना	Fortune to smile on someone
किस्मत फिरना/फूटना/सो जाना	Luck to run out
किस्मत लड़ना	1. To be lucky, to have a good run of luck 2. To be in the fray
किस्सा उठाना	To broach a subject, To start a dispute
किस्सा खड़ा करना	To create a problem, To raise an issue
किस्सा खत्म होना	Closing of a chapter
किस्सा गढ़ना	To concoct a story
कीचड़ उछालना	1. To cast aspersions on someone 2. To make disgraceful imputations to 3. To throw mud
कीचड़ फेंकना	To indulge in character assassination, To sling mud
कीचड़ में फँसना	To fall into a morass
कीड़ा, किताबी	Book-worm
कीड़े पड़ना	1. To become rotten 2. To suffer for one's black deeds

कीमत, किसी (पर)	At any cost, By all means
कीमत चुकाना	To pay up, to pay the price (for deeds)
कीमत, हर (पर)	At all costs, By any means
कुँजड़ों की लड़ाई	1. Quarrel like low-bred people 2. Quarrel over trifles
कुंजी हाथ में होना	To be under one's thumb, To hold the key to
कुंदन हो जाना, शरीर	To be restored to perfect health after illness
कुआँ खोदते ही खाई तैयार	Harm set, harm get
कुआँ खोदना	To lay a trap for
कुएँ का मेढक	1. A frog in the well 2. An unenlightened person
कुएँ झाँकना	To make all-out efforts, To search high and low
कुएँ में धकेलना	To ruin the life of somebody
कुएँ में बाँस डालना	To search frantically
कुएँ में भाँग पड़ना	One and all to have taken leave of their senses
कुएँ से प्यासा लौटना	To reach the destination and yet return disappointed
कुछ उठा न रखना	To spare no efforts
कुछ कर देना	To bewitch, To enchant, To practise black magic
कुछ कर बैठना	To take a drastic step

कुछ कह बैठना	To say something unpalatable
कुछ-का-कुछ (विपरीत, उलटा)	Something altogether different
कुछ, चाहे	Whatever may be
कुछ-न-कुछ	Something or the other
कुछ न चलना	No say (in the matter)
कुछ न पूछिए (अवर्णनीय)	1. It beggars description 2. Words fail to describe
कुछ न सूझना	To be at a loss
कुछ नहीं तो थोड़ी भली	1. Half a loaf is better than no bread 2. Something is better than nothing
कुछ समझना	To assume airs
कुछ होना (होकर रहना)	Something is bound to happen
कुढ़-कुढ़कर मरना	To fret all one's life
कुत्ता, अपनी गली में (शेर होना)	Every cock fights best on his own dunghill
कुत्ते का कुत्ता बैरी	Two of a trade seldom agree
कुत्ता घसीटी	Filthy and fruitless work
कुत्ते की मौत मरना	To die a miserable death, To die by inches
कुत्ते की दुम	1. A incorrigibly bad person 2. An inflexible and uncompromising person
कुत्ते की नींद सोना	A dog-like sleep
कुप्पा, फूलकर होना	To be beside oneself with joy
कुप्पा, मुँह होना	To be in a fit of the sulks
कुरसी का अहमक	A downright fool
कुरसी का जादू	Spell of authority

कुरसी का भूखा	Power-hungry
कुरसी तोड़ना	1. To remain in a seat of power without doing anything 2. To sit pretty idle
कुरसी पर बैठना	To be installed in a seat of authority
कुरसी सँभालना	1. To enter upon an office
कुरेद-कुरेदकर पूछना	To put probing questions
कुल उछालना	To disgrace one's family
कुल का नाम डुबोना/ कुल को कलंक लगाना	1. To bring slur on the fair name of the family 2. To tarnish the image of the family
कुलाबे मिलाना (जमीन आसमान के)	1. To build castles in the air 2. To talk of unachievable things
कूच करना	To die
कूच बोलना	To sound the departure of a troop
कूट-कूटकर भरना/भरा होना	1. To be crammed 2. To be possessed in great measure
कूड़े के दिन फिरना	Every dog has his day
कूढ़-के-कूढ़	Utterly foolish
कूदना, किसी के बल पर	1. To bask in someone else's reflected glory 2. To plume oneself on somebody else's strength
कूद पड़ना	To jump into the fray

कैंची काटना	To slip away
कैंची-सी जबान	Sharp tongue
कोख उजड़ना	Death of a woman's only child or all children
कोठे पर बैठना	To earn a living as a prostitute
कोठी खोलना	To start a business
कोठी बैठना	Failing of a business, A house to collapse
कोढ़ में खाज	1. A pimple has grown upon an ulcer 2. Onslaught of a calamity on the top of another
कोढ़ी के भी दिन फिरते हैं	Every dog has his day
कोना-कोना छान मारना	To search every nook and corner
कोना-कोना झाँकना	To avoid being face-to-face
कोने-कोने में	In every nook and cranny
कोयला हो जाना (जलकर)	1. To become envious 2. To become furious
कोर-कसर न छोड़ना / रहने देना	1. To do everything possible 2. Not to leave even a single flaw
कोरा बचना	To escape unhurt
कोरा रह जाना	To get nothing
कोरा लौटना	To return empty-handed
कोरी कल्पना	Sheer fancy
कोरी बातें करना	To indulge in empty talk
कोल्हू का बैल	Galley slave
कोल्हू के बैल की तरह पिलना	1. To keep one's nose to the grindstone

	2. To work hard and continuously
	3. To work hard like a galley slave
कोल्हू में डालकर पेरना	To torment
कोसों दूर रहना	To remain miles away from
कौआ चला हंस की चाल	Airs and graces, Borrowed plumes
कौड़ियों के मोल	At throw-away price, Dirt cheap
कौड़ी कफन न होना	To be absolutely penniless
कौड़ी काम का न होना	To be good for nothing
कौड़ी को भी न पूछना	1. To attach no value 2. To hold in no esteem 3. To treat like dirt
कौड़ी-कौड़ी को मोहताज	To be hard pressed for every farthing
कौड़ी-कौड़ी चुकाना/ भरना	To pay off to the last penny
कौड़ी-कौड़ी दाँत से पकड़ना	1. To accumulate little by little 2. To be extremely miser and stingy
कौड़ी खेलना	To gamble
कौड़ी गलत पड़ना	To miss the target
कौड़ी, दो (का)	A worthless fellow
कौड़ी भर	In a very small quantity
कौर छीनना (मुँह का)	To rob someone of his due share
कौल का पक्का	True to one's word
कौल तोड़ना	To break one's promise
कौल से फिरना / हारना	To go back on one's word

क्या कहने (खूब)	Bravo! How splendid! Well done!
क्रोध पी जाना	To suppress one's anger
क्रोध में भर जाना	To be filled with anger, To be very angry

ख

खंड-खंड करना	1. To demolish
(चकनाचूर करना)	2. To smash to pieces
खजाने, खुले	Openly, publicly
खटाई में डालना	1. To put in cold storage
	2. To shelve (matter)
खटाई में पड़ना	1. To be kept in abeyance
	2. To be shelved
खट्टा होना, जी/मन	To be disgusted
खट्टे करना, दाँत	To defeat completely,
	To make one lick the dust
खड़ा करना/होना	1. To initiate
	2. To set up, to be set up
खड़ा रखना	1. To support
	2. To maintain
खड़े पाँव	Immediately, without delay
खड़े, भाग (होना)	To escape successfully,
	To make good one's escape
खतरा मोल लेना	1. To invite danger
	2. To incur risk
खतरे की घंटी	Danger signal

खपना, मर	1. To be exhausted 2. To die
खपाना, सिर	To rack one's brains
खप्पर भरना	To give alms
खबर आना	It is reported, Report to come in
खबर उड़ाना	To spread a report, To set afloat a rumour
खबर करना	To report to
खबर लगाना	To trace out
खबर लेना	1. To enquire about 2. To look after, to watch over 3. To reprove 4. To take someone to task
खम ठोकना	To be ready to fight
खम बजाना	To challenge for a duel
खयाल में रखना	To bear in mind
खयाल से उतरना	To slip out of one's memory/ mind
खयाल से बाहर	Inconceivable, To be out of one's mind
खयाली दुनिया	World of fancies/fantasies
खयाली पुलाव पकाना	1. To amuse oneself 2. To build castles in the air
खरा उतरना	To hold water, To stand a test
खराद पर चढ़ना	To be improved
खराब करना	To corrupt, To spoil,

	To violate
खरामाँ खरामाँ चलना	To walk in a stately way, To walk with graceful ease
खरी-खरी सुनाना	1. To be outspoken 2. To call a spade a spade 3. To speak harshly
खरी-खोटी सुनाना	1. To give a bit of one's mind 2. To speak out bitter truths
खाक उड़ना	To go to rack and ruin
खाक करना	To devastate, To reduce to ashes
खाक छानना (दर-दर की) / उड़ाना	1. To knock about from pillar to post 2. To roam about aimlessly
खाक डालना	1. To bury 2. To conceal
खाक फाँकना	To roam
खाक में मिल जाना	1. To be reduced to ashes 2. To be ruined
खाक हो जाना	1. To be destroyed 2. To come to dust
खाका उड़ाना	1. To make fun of 2. To pull one's leg
खाज, कोढ़ में (होना)	1. A pimple has grown upon an ulcer 2. One trouble on the top of another
खा जाना, कच्चा	1. To burst into a fit of anger on someone

	2. To eat raw
	3. To swallow unroasted
खाट तोड़ना	To idle away one's time, To spend time mostly lying down idly
खाट (खटिया) खड़ी करना	To put someone to a great trouble
खाट पकड़ना	To be taken ill, To fall ill
खाट पर पड़ जाना / से लगना	To be bedridden
खाट से उतारना	To be on the verge of death, To take a dying man from his bed
खाता खोलना	To open an account, To start
खातिर करना	1. To beat black and blue 2. To show regard
खाना, जिसका (उसी पर गुर्राना)	To bite the hand that feeds one, To growl at one who provides food
खाना, मुँह की	1. To be beaten hollow 2. To bite the dust
खाने दौड़ना	To react violently, To behave with unwarranted aggressiveness
खाने (का) न पचना	1. To be on pins and needles 2. To be uneasy
खार खाना (खाए बैठना)	To be on the look-out for an opportunity to take revenge,

	To feel rancour against, To nurse a grudge
खार निकालना	To vent rancour
खारिज होना	To be dismissed
खाल उधेड़ना	To punish severely, To thrash soundly
खालाजी का घर होना	A place of comfort and security
खाली जाना, निशाना	To miss the mark (object)
खाली जाना, वचन	Promise to go unfulfilled
खाली लौटना	To return failing in one's mission
खाली हाथ आना	1. To return disappointed 2. To return penniless
खाली हाथ रहना	1. Empty-handed 2. Unarmed
खाली हाथ लौटना	1. To draw a blank 2. To meet with failure in one's pursuit
खिंचे-खिंचे रहना	To avoid meeting, To keep aloof
खिचड़ी पकना	1. A conspiracy to be hatched, 2. Something secret on the cards 3. Trouble to be brewed
खिचड़ी पकाना	1. To conspire 2. To hatch a plot
खिचड़ी पकाना, ढाई चावल की (अलग)	1. To consider oneself a cut above others 2. To go against general opinion in one's intentions 3. To paddle one's own canoe

खिचड़ी पकाना, बीरबल की	Something impossible
खिलवाड़ समझना	To treat as a child's play
खिलौना, हाथ का (आमोद-प्रमोद का साधन)	Playing in one's hand, Puppet in the hands of
खिल्ली उड़ाना (हँसी उड़ाना)	To make fun, To mock at, To ridicule
खिल्ली में उड़ाना	To treat as a joke
खिसियानी बिल्ली खंभा नोचे	A thrashed army resorts to rampage
खींचना, हाथ	To cease to take interest, To withdraw support
खीज निकालना	To settle a score
खीर, टेढ़ी	A hard nut to crack
खीर में नोन	A fly in the ointment
खीरा-ककड़ी समझना	To treat as insignificant
खीरे के मोल	Very cheaply, dirt cheap
खील-खील हो जाना	To be shattered to pieces
खीसें निकालना / निपोरना	To wear a grin
खुदा-खुदा करके	With extreme difficulty
खुल जाना	1. To be too familiar with 2. To come out of one's shell 3. To make free with 4. To throw off reserve
खुलना, किस्मत (भाग्य)	To have a sudden windfall of luck
खुलना, गाँठ	To remove misunderstanding
खुलना, दिमाग	Broadening of outlook
खुलना, भेद	The cat is out of the bag, The secret is out

खुला खेलना	To go at great speed, To indulge (in misdeeds) openly
खुली छूट देना	To give a free hand, To give a long rope
खुलेआम अपमान करना	To offer an affront to
खुले खजाने	1. In an open space 2. Openly, publicly, fearlessly
खुश्क होना, प्राण	To be mortally scared, To be terrified
खूँटे के बल कूदना/उछलना	1. To bask in the reflected glory 2. To depend on another's support/protection 3. To show off on the strength of another
खूँटे गाड़ना	1. To attain fame 2. To decide the limits of something 3. To draw a line somewhere
खूँटे से बाँधना, कसाई के	To expose one to the danger ahead
खून उतरना, आँखों में	To get one's blood up
खून उबलना	To make one's blood boil
खून करना	To murder
खून सवार होना, सिर पर	To be out to murder
खून का घूँट पीना	1. To suppress one's feeling 2. To swallow an insult
खून का जोश होना	Family feeling
खून का प्यासा होना	1. Intending to murder, 2. To be at daggers drawn

	3. To be thirsty for someone's blood
खून का बदला	Revenge for murder
खून के आँसू रोना	To be in terrible grief
खून चूसना	1. To exact the largest possible amount of labour from a person at the lowest possible pay
	2. To exploit to the maximum
	3. To suck blood
खून पसीना एक करना	1. To do one's utmost
	2. To strain every nerve
	3. To toil ceaselessly
खून पसीने की कमाई	1. To earn by the sweat of one's brow
	2. Hard-earned money
खून पीना	1. To be out for blood
	2. To harass non-stop
खून लगना, मुँह को	To get addicted to something
खून सफेद होना	1. Blood to turn white
	2. To be devoid of all human feelings
खून सवार होना (उन्मत्त होना)	To run amuck
खून सूखना	To be mortally terrified
खेत रहना	1. To be killed in action
	2. To fall in battle
	3. To fall wounded
खेल खिलाना	To cause harassment by crafty means

खेल खेलना	To make a crafty move
खेल खेलना, जान पर	To do something at the risk of one's life
खेल-खेल में	1. Just in fun 2. Without much effort
खेल, बाएँ हाथ का	There is nothing to it
खेल बिगड़ जाना	1. Bring one's eggs to a bad market 2. Plans to go awry
खेल बिगाड़ना	1. To spoil one's plans 2. To upset one's apple-cart
खेलना, जान पर	To risk one's life
खेलना, सिर पर मौत	Death hovering on one's head
खोज खबर लेना	To enquire about
खोज निकालना	To find a clue
खोज में रहना	To be on the look out
खोट होना, मन में	1. To be dishonest at heart 2. To bear ill-will 3. To feel rancour against someone
खोटी-खरी सुनाना	1. To give somebody a piece of one's mind 2. To scold
खोटी-सलाह	Ill-advice
खोद-खोदकर पूछना	1. To cross-examine critically 2. To question closely
खोदा पहाड़, निकली चुहिया	1. A most disappointing result 2. Mountain was in labour and mouse was produced

खोपड़ी, औंधी (मूर्ख)	1. Blockhead, foolish, stupid 2. Ill-furnished in the attic storey
खोपड़ी खुजलाना (मार खाने को जी चाहना)	1. To invite knock on one's head 2. To look for trouble
खोपड़ी खाना (बकवास से तंग करना)	1. To pester with persistent queries 2. To tease by overtalking
खोपड़ी गंजी करना	To give a severe thrashing
खोपड़ी में घुसना	To get into one's head
खोया-खोया-सा रहना	To look lost
खोलकर, जी	1. Openly 2. To one's heart's content
ख्याली पुलाव पकाना	To build castles in the air, To live in a make-believe world

गंगा, उलटी (बहाना)	To carry coals to Newcastle
गंगा नहाना	1. To achieve a goal 2. To be relieved of some great responsibility
गंगा, बहती (में हाथ धोना)	1. Make hay while the sun shines 2. Take advantage at the proper time
गंधर्व विवाह करना	To jump over the broom-stick
गजब ढाना	1. To be outrageous 2. To bewitch (by one's beauty) 3. To do wonders
गज-भर की जबान होना	1. Long tongue 2. To be over-talkative
गठरी बाँधना	To prepare for a journey
गठरी मारना	To rob
गड़प करना	To embezzle
गड्ड-मड्ड करना	To mess up
गड़े मुरदे उखाड़ना	To flog a dead horse, To rake up the old issues

गड़े मुरदे मत उखाड़ो	Let by-gones be by-gones, Let sleeping dogs lie
गढ़ जीतना/तोड़ना	To accomplish a difficult feat/ task/job
गत करना	To beat thoroughly
गत (गति) बनाना	1. To reduce to a pitiable plight 2. To spoil one's appearance
गत हो जाना	To be dead
गद्दी पर बैठना	1. To ascend the throne 2. To be enthroned 3. To hold authority
गधा खेत खाए और कुम्हार मारा जाए	To bark up a wrong tree, To denounce a wrong person
गधा होना	Long ears
गधे को अंगूरी बाग	Honey is not made for the mouth of an ass
गधे को बाप बनाना	To flatter a fool for expediency
गधे को भी घोड़ा बनाना	To make donkey run faster than the horse
गधे-घोड़े को पहचानना	To differentiate between chalk and cheese
गधे पर चढ़ना	To be humiliated
गधे पर चढ़ाना	To disgrace, to humiliate
गधे से गिरा, गुस्सा कुम्हार पर	To bark up a wrong tree
गधे से घोड़े का काम लेना	Make a silk purse out of a sow's ear, To get better results from a person than his qualities admit of
गन्ना न दे, भेली दे	Penny wise, pound foolish

गम खाना	To bear grief, To be tolerant
गया वक्त फिर हाथ नहीं आता	Time past is forever gone
गरज का यार	A fair-weather friend
गरज निकालना	To achieve one's purpose
गरज पड़ना	To be in need of
गरज बावली होना	Compelling need knows no scruples
गरज रखना	1. To aim at 2. To have an interest in
गरजते हैं वे बरसते नहीं, जो	Barking dogs seldom bite
गरदन झुकाना	To hang one's head in shame
गरदन (गरदन) नीची होना	To suffer humiliation
गरदन पर छुरी चलाना	To put one to an immense loss
गरदन पर सवार होना	To breathe down someone's neck, To embarrass by being unnecessarily present
गरदन फँसाना	1. To get involved unnecessarily 2. To stick one's neck out
गरदन मरोड़ना	To twist the neck
गरदन में हाथ डालना	To hold by the jugular
गरीब मार होना	To get the wrong sow by the ear
गरीबी में आटा गीला	A light purse is a great curse
गरेबान में मुँह डालकर देखना	To introspect, To see within oneself
गलना, दाल नहीं	Not to achieve one's end, Your wares won't sell here

गला काटना	1. To be deprived of one's dues 2. To cheat
गला घोंटना	To strangle
गला छूटना	To get rid of
गला दबाना	To exert undue influence
गला पकड़ना	To hold by the neck
गला फाड़ना	To shout very loudly
गला भर आना	1. Lump in one's throat 2. Voice choked with emotion
गलाना, शरीर	To cause one's body to decay
गली-गली मारे-मारे फिरना	To roam from place to place
गली में कुत्ता भी शेर होता है, अपनी	Every cock crows on its own dunghill
गले उतारना	To ram something down one's throat
गले का हार	A constant companion
गले के नीचे उतरना	To go down one's throat
गले न उतरना	To stick in one's throat
गले पड़ना	To force oneself upon
गले पड़ा ढोल	Someone forced upon another
गले बाँधना	Thrust thing down one's throat
गले मंढ़ना	To pass the baby, To pass the buck to
गले में हड्डी अटकना	Not to be palatable or welcome
गले लगाना	To hug
गहरा आदमी	1. A deep person 2. A person of a secretive nature
गहरा आसामी	A wealthy person

गहरा दोस्त	A close friend
गहरा हाथ मारना	1. To inflict a severe blow 2. To reap a rich harvest
गहरी घुटना/छानना	1. To be chummy 2. To be intimate with
गहरे में चलना	To make subtle moves
गहरे होना	To gain substantially, to prosper
गाँठ का खोना	To incur loss
गाँठ का पक्का	Close-fisted
गाँठ का पूरा होना	1. Fools to others, to himself a sage 2. Having money in plenty but stingy in spending
गाँठ खुलना	1. Solution of a puzzle 2. To unravel the mystery
गाँठ जोड़ना	1. To become intimate 2. To splice
गाँठ बाँध लेना	To remember life-long
गाँठ, मन की (खोलना)	To speak openheartedly
गाँठ, मन में (पड़ना)	1. Bad blood, ill-feeling 2. Having a grouse
गाँठना, मतलब	To secure a selfish end
गागर में सागर भरना	To express the maximum in the minimum words
गाज गिरना/पड़ना	A bolt from the blue, To be afflicted by a sudden calamity
गाजर-मूली समझना	To treat as insignificant
गाढ़ी छनना	To be thick with each other

गाढ़े दिन भोगना	Days of hardship, To live in hard times
गाढ़े पसीने की कमाई	Hard-earned money
गाढ़े में	In deep crisis
गाना, अपना ही	1. To blow one's own trumpet 2. To indulge in self-praise
गाल, काल के (में जाना)	To be devoured by death
गाल फुलाना (रूठना)	1. To be haughty 2. To sulk
गाल बजाना	1. To boast 2. To chatter 3. To grab
गाली पर उतर आना	1. To come down to calling names 2. To stoop to vituperation
गिन-गिनकर कदम रखना	To proceed extra-cautiously
गिन-गिनकर गालियाँ देना	To burst into a volley of abuses
गिनती गिनाना	Nominal
गिनती में आना	1. To be on the map 2. To deserve inclusion
गिनती में न लाना	1. Not to take into account 2. To consider as insignificant
गिनती में लाना	1. To be well known 2. To put on the map
गिनना, दिन	1. To count days 2. To pass time somehow or the other
गिने-चुने	Selected
गिरते हैं शहसवार ही मैदाने जंग में	A good marksman may miss the mark

गिर-पड़कर पाना	To get with a great deal of difficulty
गिरह पड़ना	A misunderstanding to arise
गिरह बाँधना	To keep in mind
गीत गाना	1. To tell a long tale 2. To sing the praises
गुजारा करना	1. To keep the pot boiling 2. To make both ends meet
गुड़ की-सी बातें	Sweet words
गुड़ खाना और गुलगुलों से परहेज	To strain at a gnat and swallow a camel
गुड़, गूँगे का	To have an experience that defies expression
गुड़-गोबर कर देना	To make a hash of, to mess up, to ruin, to spoil utterly
गुड़ दिखाकर ढेला मारना	1. To frustrate one's hopes after raising them 2. To offer a caress and give a stab
गुड़ियों का खेल (आसान काम)	1. A child's paly 2. An easy job 3. Matter taken lightly
गुदड़ी का लाल	A gem in refuse, a jewel in rags
गुबार निकालना	To release pent-up emotions
गुल खिलना	Unexpected and interesting development in an affair
गुल खिलाना	1. To cause disturbance 2. To do something unexpected and untoward

गुलछर्रे उड़ाना	To enjoy oneself, To live carefree life, To revel with abandon
गुस्सा थूक देना	To be pacified, To forgive and forget
गुस्सा नाक पर रहना	To be short-tempered
गुस्सा पी ज़ाना	To suppress one's anger
गुस्सा भड़क उठना	To blaze up
गूँगे का गुड़	An experience beyond words
गूँगे का सपना देखना	To dream, but be dumb
गूदा, बात का (निकालना)	To get to the core of a matter
गूलर का फूल माँगना	Cry for the moon
गेरुए कपड़े पहनने से कोई साधु नहीं हो जाता	It is not the hood that makes the monk
गोटी जमना/बैठना	Showing promise of success
गोटी पिटना	A plan to come to a naught
गोटी बिठाना	To succeed in carrying one's scheme through
गोटी लाल होना	A move that yielded success
गोटी हाथ से जाना	1. To miss an opportunity 2. A plan to fail
गोड़ टूटना	1. To be totally exhausted 2. To be utterly disappointed
गोद देना	To give one's child for being adopted
गोद पसारना	Begging
गोद बैठना	To be adopted
गोद भरना	1. To be blessed with motherhood

	2. To fill the lap of a girl with auspicious articles before her marriage
गोद में डालना	To give a child for adoption
गोद लेना	To adopt a child
गोद सूनी रहना	To be childless
गोबर गणेश (मूर्ख, मंदबुद्धि)	1. Beetle-brain
	2. Blockhead
	3. Dunder-head
गोरख धंधा	1. Indirect and secret agencies
	2. Wheels within wheels
गोल करना	1. To evade
	2. To remove something clandestinely
गोल बात कहना	1. To deliver ambiguous statement
	2. To equivocate
गोल रहना	1. To be absent
	2. To remain non-committal
गोल हो जाना	To take french leave
गोल होना	To slip away
गोलमोल जवाब देना	To answer evasively
गोलियाँ, कच्ची, न खेलना	Not to be befooled

घ

घटाटोप छाना	1. Darkness to prevail 2. Gathering of dark clouds
घड़ा, चिकना	A brazenly shameless person
घड़ियाँ गिनना	1. To be on death-bed 2. To wait anxiously
घड़ी में घड़ियाल (क्षणभंगुर जीवन)	Life is uncertain
घड़ों पानी पड़ना	1. To be subjected to extreme humiliation 2. To blush with shame, to feel shame
घन-चक्कर में आना	To get into a predicament
घमंडी का सिर नीचा	Pride hath a fall
घर आबाद करना	To get married
घर उजड़ना	To be ruined
घर करना (दिल में)	To be embedded, to settle
घर का भेदी लंका ढावे	Traitors are the worst enemies
घर की खेती	Within one's reach
घर को सिर पर उठाना	To make a hell of a noise in the house

घर फूँककर तमाशा देखना	To rejoice at one's own cost
घर फोड़ना	To create a rift in a family
घर बसाना	To marry
घर बिगाड़ना	To ruin the family
घर बैठना	1. To be out of work 2. To be somebody's mistress 3. The house to cave in
घर बैठे	1. Easily 2. Without any effort
घर सिर पर उठा लेना	To raise a roof
घर से बेघर करना	To render homeless
घाट का, न घर का न	Good for nothing
घाट-घाट का पानी पीना	To gather varied experience by going from pillar to post
घाट मारना	To smuggle
घाट लगना	To reach one's destination
घात ताकना	To look for an opportunity
घात में बैठना	To lie in ambush
घात लगना	Opportunity to be found
घात लगाना	1. To lie in ambush, 2. To lie in wait
घाल-मेल करना	To mix up
घाल-मेल रखना	To be on intimate terms
घाव पर नमक छिड़कना	To add insult to injury
घाव हरा हो आना	A lingering sorrow to revive
घास खोदना	1. To undertake a worthless job 2. To engage oneself in a trifling work 3. To do something pointless

घी का कुप्पा लुढ़कना	A loss to be sustained
घी के दिए जलाना	1. To feel extremely jubilant 2. To prosper
घी खिचड़ी होना	1. To be closely intimate 2. To be hand in glove with
घी दूध की नदी बहाना	To wallow in riches
घी, पाँचों उँगलियाँ (में होना)	1. To gain immensely 2. To revel in wealth
घुंडी खोलना, मन की	To unburden one's heart
घुट-घुटकर मर जाना	To die a lingering death, To fret out one's life
घुटना, खूब	1. To be chummy 2. Very close
घुटने टेकना	1. To acknowledge superiority of 2. To admit defeat by 3. To kneel in entreaty to 4. To submit to 5. To surrender 6. To yield to
घुटने में सिर देना	1. To be engrossed in some deep thought 2. To hide one's head in shame or grief
घुटनों के बल चलना	To walk on all fours, to crawl
घुट्टी में पड़ना	To have something as a part of one's nature
घुल-घुलकर बातें करना (घनिष्ठता से बातें करना)	1. To have friendly talks 2. To sit tete-a-tete 3. To speak intimately

घुल-घुलकर मरना	To die by inches
घुल-मिलकर रहना	To live in perfect harmony
घुसकर बैठना	To hide oneself inside, To infiltrate
घूँट पीना, लहू का	1. To suffer a humiliating experience 2. To suppress one's rage
घूमना, सिर	To be drowsy, To be tipsy
घूरे के दिन फिरना, बारह बरस बाद	Every dog has his day, No man is always unlucky
घेर-घार करना	1. To enclose 2. To entrap 3. To surround
घेरा डालना	To blockade, To lay siege to
घेरे में पड़ना	To be surrounded by
घोटा लगाना	To learn by heart
घोड़े पर चढ़े आना	To be in undue haste
घोड़े बेचकर सोना	1. To be relieved of all anxieties 2. To have a deep and carefree sleep
घोलकर पी जाना	To assimilate thoroughly
घोलना जहर, काम में	1. To make someone's life miserable 2. To put a spanner/spike in the work

च

चंगुल में आना	To fall into someone's clutches
चंगुल में फँसना / पड़ना	1. To be entrapped 2. To fall into the trap
चंपत हो जाना, (गायब हो जाना)	1. To run away 2. To take to one's heels 3. To vanish into thin air
चकमा खाना	To be cheated/deceived
चकमा देना	1. To cheat 2. To dodge, to hoodwink
चकमे में आना / पड़ना	1. To be hoodwinked 2. To fall a victim to one's trickery
चकरा जाना, दिमाग / सिर	1. To be confused 2. To be nonplussed
चक्कर काटना	To revolve
चक्कर खाना	To be confounded
चक्कर चलना	1. To carry on something fishy 2. Something going on in between the two
चक्कर पड़ना	To be in a mess
चक्कर मारना	To visit sporadically

चक्कर में डालना	1. To be deceived 2. To make confusion worse confounded
चक्कर में पड़ना / लगाना	To be puzzled, To get involved in a mess
चक्की चलाना	To work laboriously
चक्की पीसना	To work rigorously
चक्की में पिसना	To toil hard
चखना, मजे (का)	To stew in one's own juice
चचा निकलना	To surpass in cleverness
चटक जाना, आपस में	1. To develop a dispute 2. To fall out
चट कर जाना	1. To consume ravenously 2. To embezzle
चट-पट हो जाना	To die suddenly
चटनी करना	To bruise
चटनी होना	To be completely exhausted
चट्टे-बट्टे, एक ही थैली के	Birds of the same feather, Chips of the same block
चढ़ बनना	1. To gain ground 2. To prosper
चढ़ बैठना	To overpower
चढ़ते सूर्य को नमस्कार करना	1. To adore the rising sun 2. To be on the winning side 3. To curry new power's favour
चने (बहु.) चबवाना, नाकों/ लोहे के	1. To torment 2. To give a gruelling time
चपत देना	1. To give a blow 2. To put one to loss

चपत पड़ना / लगना	To incur loss
चपेट में आना	1. To be injured 2. To be threatened by 3. To fall a victim to
चप्पा-चप्पा छानना	To search every nook and corner
चबा-चबाकर बात करना	To talk haltingly and with reserve
चमड़ी उधेड़ना	To beat black and blue
चरखा चलाना	1. To speak too much without stopping 2. To spin a long story
चरण चूमना	1. To flatter 2. To kowtow
चरबी छाना	To become arrogant and self-centred
चर्चा चलाना	To broach a subject
चर्चा होना / फैल जाना	1. To be the talk of the town 2. To take air (become known)
चल देना	To slip away
चल निकलना	1. To get going 2. To make good progress
चल बसना	To die
चलता करना	1. To dispose of 2. To send away
चलता बनना	To slip away
चस्का होना	To be addicted to
चाँद चढ़ना	A good fortune to dawn
चाँद, चार (लगना)	To have a feather added to one's cap
चाँद पर थूकना / धूल डालना	To bring disgrace on oneself

चाँद में भी दाग है	1. Every bean has its black 2. No one is without faults
चाँद पर बाल न छोड़ना	1. To beat mercilessly 2. To despoil one utterly 3. To rob 4. To thrash
चाँदनी, चार दिन की	1. A short-lived happiness 2. Ephemeral glamour 3. Flashy glory 4. Nine day's wonder
चाँदी का जूता	Bribe
चाँदी काटना	To be minting money
चाँदी की वर्षा होना	Oodles of money, Superabundance of money
चाँदी के पहिए लगाना	1. To grease the palm 2. To make things go smoothly by bribery 3. To oil the wheels
चाँदी होना	To be flourishing, To have all round gains
चाक करना	To tear apart
चादर उतारना	To disgrace a woman
चादर ओढ़ाना	To marry a widow
चादर काली होना	1. To be ashamed 2. To disgrace oneself
चादर देखकर पाँव पसारना	Cut your coat according to your cloth
चादर से बाहर पाँव फैलाना	To be extravagant, To spend beyond one's means

चाबी भरना	To instigate
चार अक्षर पढ़ना	To have a smattering knowledge
चार कदम	A short distance
चार चाँद लगना	1. To enhance one's reputation 2. To have one more feather to one's cap
चार चाँद लगाना	To add lustre to one's glory
चारपाई पर पड़ना	To be confined to bed
चार पैसे होना	To have sizeable wealth
चार सौ बीस होना	A smooth operator, A trickster
चाल, घर की	Family tradition
चाल पकड़ना	1. To become current 2. To catch up with 3. To detect the trick 4. To keep pace with
चाल में फँसना	1. To be deceived 2. To walk into the trap of
चालू आदमी	Smart sharper
चाह, जहाँ (वहाँ राह)	Where there is a will, there is a way
चिंता चिता समान	Care killed the cat
चिकना घड़ा होना	To be insensitive to criticism, blame etc., To be thick-skinned
चिकनी-चुपड़ी बातें करना	1. To cajole 2. To curry favour 3. To flatter for gaining favour
चिकने घड़े की तरह होना	Having absolutely no effect,

	Like water off duck's back
चिट्ठा, कच्चा (खोलना)	To reveal dubious dealings
चिड़िया का दूध	Some thing impossible/absurd, Unreal thing
चिड़िया फँसाना	To entrap someone (a wealthy person)
चिड़िया, सोने की	1. El dorado 2. A wealthy person/country
चित कर देना	To overpower, To render helpless
चित्त उचटना	1. To be indifferent to, to lose interest in 2. To suffer from ennui
चित्त गिराना, चारों खाने	1. Tyrannize over 2. Utterly subdue
चित्त देना	To be attentive, To pay heed to
चित्त पर चढ़ना	To be ever present in the mind, To be impressed on the mind
चित्त बँटना	The mind to be distracted
चित्त में बैठना / जमना	1. To be always in the mind 2. To be in love with
चित्त में बैठाना	1. To instil in the mind 2. To set one's heart on
चित्त लगना	To make oneself at home
चित्त से उतरना	To be neglected, To lose interest in
चित्त हो जाना	To be overpowered, To fall on the back

चिनगारी छूटना, आँखों से (क्रोध से लाल आँख होना)	Eyes to be red with anger
चिनगारी छोड़ना	1. To emit sparks 2. To make an incendiary remark
चिनगारी डालना / लगाना	To make the fur fly, To stir up trouble
चिपके रहना	To stick to a post
चिराग गुल होना	A family line to be extinguished
चिराग बुझना	The light of the family is extinguished
चिराग तले अँधेरा होना	Nearer the church, farther from God
चिराग लेकर ढूँढ़ना	To search with all the care at one's command
चिराग, घी के (जलना)	To make great rejoicing
चिरौरी करना (मनाना)	To supplicate
चिलम-तंबाकू बंद करना	To cease to have social intercourse, To freeze out, To ostracise
चिलम भरना	To dance attendance upon, To serve (one)
चीं-चप्पड़ करना	To protest explicitly
चीं बुलाना	To make one admit defeat
चीं बोल जाना	To show utter helplessness
चीं बोलना	To admit defeat
चींटी की चाल चलना	1. To move at a snail's pace, 2. To walk very slowly

चींटी के पर निकलना	To be heading for trouble/ death, To be too big for one's boots, To outgrow oneself
चींटे होना, गुड़	To consort closely
चीज पर दाँत होना	To have an eye to, To set one's heart on
चील झपट्टा मारना	To snatch violently
चुटकियों में उड़ाना	1. To make fun of 2. To outwit 3. To pass off in a light-hearted manner
चुटकियों में काम करना	To perform a task easily
चुटकी लेना	To make a sarcastic remark
चुटिया हाथ में होना	To be under one's complete control
चुनचुने लगना	To be irritated
चुप्पी साधना	1. To keep breath to cool porridge 2. To abstain from talk
चुपड़ी बात करना, चिकनी	To curry favour, To flatter
चुराना, आँख	To look furtively at
चुल्लू-चुल्लू बढ़ना / साधना	1. To grow gradually rich 2. Slow and steady wins the race
चुल्लू-भर पानी में डूब मरना	To be awfully ashamed
चुस्त, गवाह (मुद्दई सुस्त)	1. No longer active when one's activity is most needed

	2. Witness active, defendent inactive
	3. Bridegroom's men to be more keen on marriage than the groom himself
चुहिया मारकर गोबर सुँघाना	He breaks his head and then buys a plaster
चूँ-चूँ का मुरब्बा	Hotch-potch of heterogeneous elements
चूँ-चूँ न करना	To acquiesce cravenly without any protest
चूड़ियाँ टूटना	To become a widow
चूड़ियाँ ठंडी करना / तोड़ना	To break one's bangles on the death of one's husband (Hindu wife)
चूड़ी पहनना	1. To become effeminate
	2. To behave like a woman
	3. To remarry (widow)
चूड़ी पहनाना	To marry a widow
चूना फेरना	To nullify, to undo, to whitewash
चूना लगाना	1. To cheat a gullible person of his money
	2. To delude
	3. To fleece one without mercy
	4. To swindle
चूर होना / हो जाना	To be totally exhausted
चूल्हे में पड़ना / जाना	To go to hell, to go to the devil
चूल्हे से निकलकर भाड़ में पड़ना	Out of frying pan into the fire

चेहरा उतरना / बुझना	To be downcast, to be very dejected
चेहरा खिल उठना	To cheer up
चेहरा, बुझा	Gloomy face
चेहरा भाँपना	To read one's expression
चेहरा सफेद होना	To lose the lustre of the face
चेहरे पर हवाइयाँ उड़ना	To turn pale, To wear a long face
चैन की बंशी बजाना	1. To be comfortably placed 2. To enjoy oneself thoroughly
चैन गँवाना	To lose mental peace
चैन पड़ना	To feel relieved
चोंच लड़ाना	To lock horns with, To squabble over
चोंचें होना, दो-दो	A verbal duel, To have a short wordy duel, A squabble to break out between
चोचला दिखाना	To display coquetry, To put on airs
चोट करना	To strike
चोट-पर-चोट करना	To strike in quick succession
चोट लगना	To be injured
चोटी दबना	To be under obligation
चोटी हाथ में आना	To come into or to be in another's power
चोर का साथी गिरहकट	Birds of a feather flock together
चोर की दाढ़ी में तिनका	Guilty conscience needs no excuse
चोर-चोर मौसेरे भाई	1. Dogs don't eat dogs

	2. There is honour among thieves
चोर, मन में (बैठना)	To have suspicion in mind
चोर से कहे चोरी कर, शाह से कहे जागता रह	To run with the hare and hunt with the hounds
चोरी का गुड़ मीठा	Forbidden fruits are always sweet
चोरी का धन मोरी में	Ill got, ill spent
चोरी-छिपे (चोरी-चोरी)	Clandestinely, surreptitiously
चोरी लगना	To be charged with theft
चोरी लगाना	To charge with theft
चोला छोड़ना	To give up the ghost, To kick the bucket, To leave the mortal frame (To die)
चोला बदलना (अवसरवादी बनना)	1. To be a turncoat 2. To be reborn
चोली दामन का नाता / साथ	A close association, Cheek by jowl
चौकड़ी भूलना	To be utterly confounded, To lose one's dash
चौड़ी-लंबी (बातें करना)	To talk big/tall
चौड़े में बैठा रह जाना	To be utterly ruined
चौपट करना	To corrupt, To ruin, to spoil
चौबे गए छब्बे बनने, रह गए दुबे	1. Go for wool and come home shorn 2. Have the tables turned on oneself 3. The camel going to seek horns, lost his ears

छँटे-छँटे फिरना	To hold oneself aloof from
छक्का-पंजा	Designs,
	Manoeuvrings,
	Tactics
छक्का भूलना	1. To be at a loss
	2. To be completely baffled
	3. To be out of one's wits
छक्के छुड़ा देना	1. To bring one to one's knees
	2. To take the wind from one's sails
	3. To vanquish completely
छक्के छूटना	1. To be at one's wits end
	2. To be vanquished and harassed
	3. To meet one's waterloo
छठी का खाया-पिया निकालना	To thrash soundly
छठी का दूध याद आना (भारी संकट पड़ना)	To be placed in an extremely helpless and painful position
छठी का दूध याद दिलाना	1. To beat (someone) severely
	2. To reduce one to complete helplessness
छठे-छमाही	Once in a blue moon,

	Rarely, very seldom
छनना, गहरी	On very intimate terms,
	To be hand in glove with,
	To be thick with
छपते-छपते	Stop press
छप्पन छुरी	A smart/sharp woman
छप्पर टूट पड़ना	1. A bolt from the blue
	2. A sudden calamity to befall
छप्पर पर रखना / धरना	1. To consider insignificant
	2. To postpone consideration of
	3. To treat as worthless
छप्पर फाड़कर देना	1. A windfall
	2. To bestow plentifully as a God-send
छलनी, कलेजा (कर देना)	To prick the heart
छलनी में पानी भरना	1. To square the circle
	2. To try the impossible
छलनी हो जाना	To be battered
छलनी होना	To be worn out
छाँटना, बातें	To talk tall
छाँह न छूने देना	Not to allow any one to come anywhere near one's possession
छाँह से दूर रहना	To keep scrupulously away from someone
छाज बोले सो बोले छलनी क्या बोले	Pot calling the kettle black
छाती उमगना / उमड़ना	To be deeply touched,
	To rejoice
छाती कूटना	To grieve, to wait

छाती छलनी होना	To feel extremely hurt
छाती जलाना	To be a source of envy
छाती ठंडी होना	To be assuaged, To get soothing satisfaction
छाती ठोककर कहना	To make a display of complete self-assurance
छाती ठोकना	To announce one's determination to do something
छाती तले रखना	To guard closely
छाती तानना	1. To confront fearlessly, 2. To pick up the gauntlet
छाती पकड़कर रह जाना	To be left helpless
छाती, पत्थर की (करना)	To be prepared to endure the greatest hardship, To prepare oneself to face the worst
छाती पर चढ़ना	To keep on pestering
छाती पर पत्थर रखना	To endure patiently
छाती पर बाल होना	To be able to be relied upon, To have manly traits
छाती पर मूँग दलना	To give one a hard time
छाती पर सवार होना	To be ever present to annoy
छाती पर साँप लोटना	To become jealous, To burn with envy
छाती पीटना	To repent
छाती फटना	To feel insufferable envy
छाती फूलना	To be happy and proud
छाती भरना	To be greatly moved
छाती लगाना	1. To embrace

	2. To fondle
छान मारना	To search everywhere
छाप डालना	To make an impression on
छाप पड़ना (की)	To have an impact of
छिपा रुस्तम	A dark horse
छींकते ही नाक कटना	To be over-penalised for a petty fault
छींक होना	A bad omen
छींटा कसना	To cast aspersions on someone
छींटाकशी करना	Casting aspersions, Passing sarcastic remarks
छी-छी/ छी-छी करना	1. To express dislike 2. Shame!
छुट्टी कर देना	To discharge, to dismiss
छुट्टी देना	To grant leave
छुरी चलाना	To cause pain, To do calculated harm
छुरी, मीठी	A cheat in friend's garb, A secret enemy, A sweetened dagger
छुरे, उलटे (मूँड़ना)	To treat as an utter idiot
छूत उतारना (की)	To free from the spell of some evil spirit, To remove the effect of contact
छू-मंतर होना	To vanish into thin air
छोंक भी न होना	To be a chicken-feed, To be utterly inadequate
छोटा, दिल (करना)	To feel disheartened
छोटा होना	To feel small, To lose prestige

जंग लगना	To be ineffective, To go into disuse
जंगल की आग की तरह फैलना	To spread like wild fire
जंगल जाना	To go out to relieve oneself
जंगल में मंगल	Paradise in wilderness
जंगल में मंगल मनाना	To enjoy even in solitude
जंजाल, जी का	A troublesome person / matter
जख्म ताजा कर देना	To revive an old wound
जख्म पर नमक छिड़कना	To add insult to the injury, To add to one's agony
जग-हँसाई	To be an object of ridicule
जगह से होना	To be in proper place
जटा-जूट (जटा समूह)	Matted hair rolled up over the head
जड़ खोदना	To inflict heavy damage, To pull up one's roots, To strike at the root of
जड़ जमना	To establish oneself firmly
जड़ जमाना	1. To consolidate one's position 2. To lay the foundation

जड़ पकड़ना	1. To establish 2. To take root
जड़ में होना	To be at the bottom of
जड़ हिला देना	To shake the foundations of
जन्म गँवाना	1. To lead life unworthy of human beings 2. To waste one's life
जन्म डुबोना	To ruin one's life
जब तक साँस, तब तक आस	As long as there is life, there is hope, Hope sustains life
जबान का कड़वा	Bitter-tongued
जबान का मीठा	Sweet-tongued
जबान काटना	To interrupt the speech of
जबान कैंची की तरह चलाना	1. To have a long tongue 2. To talk garrulously
जबान को लगाम देना	To bridle one's tongue
जबान खींच लेना	1. To deal with severely for talking insolently 2. To pull out one's tongue
जबान चलाना	1. To be abusive 2. To become vocal, to speak out, to talk impudently 3. To wag one's tongue
जबान दबाकर कहना	To whisper
जबान देना	To commit oneself, To give words, To promise
जबान न होना	To be reticent,

	To talk too little
जबान निकालना	To use foul language
जबान पकड़ना	To insist on the fulfilment of one's word
जबान पर चढ़ना	1. To be on the tip of one's tongue 2. To be subject of talk
जबान पर ताला पड़ना	1. To be rendered speechless 2. To be struck dumb 3. To be unable to speak due to some constraint
जबान पर न लाना	Not even to mention
जबान पर लाना	To mention
जबान पर होना	To be on the tongues of the people
जबान पलटना	To go back on one's word
जबान बंद करना	To hush, to shush, to silence
जबान बदलना	To change one's stance
जबान बिगड़ जाना	To come to abusive language
जबान में लगाम न होना	To have an uncontrolled tongue
जबान लड़ाना	To enter into vociferous arguments
जबान सँभालकर बोलना	To have a civil tongue in one's head
जबान हारना	To give one's word
जबान हिलाना	1. To make a request 2. To speak out
जमकर खाना	To eat gluttonously, To eat to the full

जमकर बातें करना	To talk whole-heartedly, To talk without reserve
जमकर बैठना	1. To settle down 2. To sit for long hours at a stretch
जमाना देखना	1. To have all sorts of experience 2. To have seen the world through and through
जमाना देखे होना	To be widely experienced
जमाना बदल जाना	The tide to have taken a turn, The times have changed
जमाना लद जाना	Those times have gone
जमाने का दस्तूर	Spirit of the times
जमाने की गर्दिश	1. Revolution of the wheel of time 2. Vicissitudes of fortune
जमाने की पुकार	1. Call of the times 2. Need of the hour
जमाने की मार	1. Buffets of fate 2. Frowns of fortune
जमाने की हवा	The trend of the age
जमाने के साथ चलना	To go with the tide, To keep pace/move with the times
जमीन आसमान एक करना	To leave no stone unturned To move heaven and earth
जमीन आसमान का फरक होना	A world of difference
जमीन आसमान के कुलाबे मिलाना	1. To boast wildly, to talk tall 2. To bring heaven and earth together

	3. To try to connect things totally unconnected with each other
जमीन तैयार करना	To prepare the ground
जमीन दिखाना	1. To defeat in wrestling
	2. To knock down flat
जमीन पर पैर न रखना	To be puffed with pride,
	To feel elated
जमीन, पाँव तले की (खिसकना)	To be stunned out of one's wits
जमीन में गड़ जाना / समाना	1. To feel deeply ashamed
	2. To hang one's head in shame
जमे रहना	To hold one's ground
जरा-जरा-सी बातें	Petty things,
	Trifles
जरा भर	Least
जल-जलकर मरना	To die in agonising jealousy
जल-जलकर राख हो जाना / कोयला हो जाना	To be consumed to ashes out of sheer jealousy
जलती आग में कूदना	To burn one's fingers knowingly,
	To risk one's life deliberately
जलती आग में घी डालना	To add fuel to the fire
जलना, हाथ (होम करते)	To suffer as a reward for doing good
जल-भुन जाना	To seethe with anger
जल मरना	1. To be seared by emotion
	2. To feel insufferably jealous
जला-जलाकर मारना	To tease one to death
जला-भुना	1. Fretting and fuming
	2. Inflamed with anger

जली-कटी सुनाना	To make biting and stinging remarks
जलूस / जुलूस निकालना (किसी का)	To subject one to public ridicule
जले को जलाना	To add fuel to the fire
जले पर नमक छिड़कना	To add insult to injury
जले फफोले फोड़ना	To give vent to accumulated wrath
जल्दी का काम शैतान का	Haste makes waste
जवानी का आलम	Stage of youthfulness
जवानी, नई (माँझा ढीला)	Young age, old ways
जवानी फटी पड़ना	To burst with youthfulness
जवाब तलब करना	Call to account (to reprimand)
जहन्नुम में जाना	To be doomed
जहर उगलना	1. To dip one's pen in gall 2. To speak spitefully
जहर का घूँट पीना (क्रोध को प्रकट न होने देना)	To endure a bitter reverse, to suppress anger
जहर की पुड़िया	1. A bundle of mischief 2. A constant cause of misery
जहर पीकर रह जाना	To swallow an insult calmly
जहाँ चाह, वहाँ राह	Where there is a will, there is a way
जहाँ फूल, वहाँ काँटा	Every rose has thorns
जहाज का पंछी	One who has only one habitat
जाके पाँव न फटी बिवाई वह क्या जाने पीर पराई	The wearer knows where the shoe pinches
जादू, आँखों में (होना)	Having charm in eyes
जादू कर देना	To cast a spell on

जादू वह जो सिर पर चढ़कर बोले	The means that achieve the end are the best means
जान आँखों में आ जाना	To be on the point of death
जान आफत में आना	To be in hot waters
जान का जंजाल	A source of trouble
जान की बाजी लगाना	To risk one's life
जान के लाले पड़ना	To be in an irretrievably risky position, To come into mortal peril
जान को पड़ना	1. To get on one's nerves 2. To pester
जान को जान न समझना	To be always ready to risk one's life
जान खपाना	To exhaust oneself in arduous work, To tire oneself out
जान खाना	To tease constantly
जान छुड़ाना	To get out of difficulty
जान छूटना	To get rid of
जान जोखिम में पड़ना	To be in jeopardy
जान देना (के लिए)	To sacrifice one's life
जान पर खेलना / आ जाना	To risk one's life,
जान मारना	To exert to the utmost
जान मुट्ठी में होना	To have (someone) at one's mercy
जान बची और लाखों पाए	1. Dutch comfort 2. However bad the evil which has fallen you, a worse is still conceivable

	3. Life is better than gold
जान में जान आना	To heave a sigh of relief
जान लड़ा देना	To spare no effort on one's part
जान सूखना	To be scared out of one's wits
जान से बेजार होना	To be awfully tired of life,
	To be tiresomely sick of life
जान हथेली पर लिए फिरना	To be ever ready to stake one's life,
	To fight with a rope round one's neck
जामा पहनाना, अमली	1. To execute into action
	2. To implement
	3. To translate into reality
जामे में फूला न समाना	To be unable to contain oneself with delight
जामे से बाहर होना	To lose control over oneself in rage
जाल[१] करना	To fabricate
जाल[२] डालना	To cast a net
	To prearrange circumstances usually secretly and unfairly
जाल फैलाना	To lay a trap
जाल बिछाना	1. To set up a network
	2. To try to ensnare
जाल रचना	To plot
जाल, शब्द	Jugglery of words
जिगर का टुकड़ा	Apple of one's eye,
	Dearly loved child
जिगर के टुकड़े होना	To be shattered to pieces

जिगर थामकर बैठना	To be in an unbearable suspense, To be in for a shock
जिगरी दोस्त (अंतरंग मित्र)	A bosom friend
जितना पैसा, उतना ही और की चाह	Plenty is the mother of want
जितने मुँह उतनी बातें	Many Men, Many minds
जिद पर आना	To adopt a stubborn attitude
जिस पत्तल में खाना उसी में छेद करना	To bite the hand that feeds one, To turn against one's benefactor
जिसका काज उसी को साजे	1. A cobbler should stick to his last 2. Every shoe fits not every foot
जिहाद बोलना	To launch a crusade
जी आना, पर	To fall in love with
जी उकताना	To be fed up
जी उचटना	To cease to have interest in some place
जी उड़ा-उड़ा रहना	To have a feeling of restlessness
जी ऊबना	To be bored, to be fed up
जी कच्चा करना	To be disheartened, To lose heart
जी कड़ा करना	To prepare oneself for any eventuality
जी का गुब्बार निकालना	To let off one's steam, To release one's pent-up feelings
जी का जंजाल	1. Crashing bore 2. Tough going 3. Troublesome
जी की जी में रहना / रह जाना	1. A desire to remain unfulfilled

	2. A thing that one wanted to say or do but could not get a chance for it
जी को मारना	To practise self-denial, To suppress desire
जी खट्टा होना	To be disgusted, To be offended
जी खपाना	To overwork
जी खोलकर	Freely, wholeheartedly, without any reserve
जी घबराना	To be uneasy, to feel nervous
जी चलना	To be tempted to
जी चुराना (काम से)	To shirk (work)
जी छोटा करना	To lose heart
जी जलाना	To eat one's heart out
जी-जान से	Heart and soul, Whole-heartedly, To make all-out efforts
जी-जान से काम करना	To work to the best of one's ability
जी टूट जाना	To be frustrated, To be heart-broken
जी ठंडा होना	To be finally satisfied
जी डूबना	To be depressed, To faint, To sink
जी तरसना	To long for, to pine for, to yearn for To be in dire want (of)
जी-तोड़ कोशिश करना	To knuckle down to it,

	To leave no stone unturned
जी दुखाना	To cause grief to, To hurt one's feelings
जी धँसना	The heart to palpitate
जी पिघल जाना	To be moved by compassion
जी बहलाना	To amuse, to recreate
जी भरकर	To one's heart's content
जी भर जाना	To be deeply moved, To be fed up
जी मर जाना	To cease to have zest for life
जी में आना	To feel like doing something
जी में जलना	To envy
जी में जी आना	To be reassured, To heave a sigh of relief
जी लगाना	To concentrate, To feel at home or easy at some place
जी ललचाना	To make one's mouth water, To yearn for
जी लुभाना	To captivate the heart
जी लोटना	To be passionately charmed by
जी से उतर जाना	To lose all respect
जी हट जाना	To become averse to
जी हारना	1. To be depressed 2. To be disheartened
जी हिलना	To have one's heart in one's mouth
जीत जाना, आसानी से	To win hands down
जीती मक्खी निगलना	To connive at something wrong

जीते-जी	In one's life-time
जीना दूभर करना	To make life miserable
जीना हराम करना	To make one's life a hell
जीभ का कड़ुवा, मन का उजला	His bark is worse than his bite
जीभ काटना	To hold tongue between the teeth to express surprise/ repentance
जीभ के तले जीभ होना	To be double tongued, To blow hot and cold
जीभ पर सरस्वती बसना	1. To deliver a spell-binding speech 2. To say things that eventually come true
जीभ हिलाना	To speak out
जीवन क्षणभंगुर है	All between cradle and coffin is uncertain
जुकाम, मेढ़की को	1. An important work being attempted by an unimportant person, 2. To take to queer ways
जुगत (जुगाड़) का आदमी बनना	To be a resourceful man
जुगत भिड़ाना / बैठाना	To manoeuvre
जुगाड़ करना / लगाना / लड़ाना	To manage
जुलूस में चलना	To march in a procession
जूँ, कानों पर (न रेंगना)	To be deaf to all arguments, To pay no heed at all
जूझ पड़ना	To jump into the fray
जूता उठाना	To be ready to give a shoe-beating

जूता खाना	To be treated insultingly
जूताखोर	Shameless, mean
जूता चलना	1. Exchange of shoe-blows, 2. Vindictive quarrel
जूता चलवाना	1. To create ill-will among people 2. To incite people to quarrel 3. To set people together by the ears 4. To set persons at loggerheads
जूता मारना	1. To hit by a shoe 2. To retaliate by insulting
जूती उसी के सिर, जिसकी	To return evil for evil
जूती मियाँ के सिर, मियाँ की	To return blow for blow, To turn a man's battery against himself
जूती का यार	1. A person whose demeanour always provokes reproof 2. One who understands only the language of rod 3. One who works when driven hard
जूते की नोक पर मारना	To treat with contempt
जूते खाना	To suffer humiliation
जूते चाटना	To flatter, To lick someone's shoes
जूते पड़ना	To be humiliated
जूते सिर पर रखकर भागना	To take to one's heels
जूते से खबर लेना / पूजा करना	To attack with insulting language, To beat with shoes

जेब खाली होना	To be penniless
जेब गरम करना/होना	1. To bribe, To grease one's palms 2. To have ample money
जेल की हवा खाना	To be behind the bars
जैसा देश-वैसा भेष	While in Rome, do as the Romans do
जैसा बोओगे वैसा काटोगे	As you sow, so shall you reap
जैसी करनी-वैसी भरनी	Drink as you have brewed
जैसी-की-तैसी करना	To put one in one's place
जैसी चाह वैसा मन	The wish is father of the thought
जैसे-का-तैसा	As it was
जैसे-को-तैसा	Tit for tat, To pay one in his own coin To return like for like
जैसे नागनाथ, वैसे साँपनाथ	Difference is merely nominal, To have nothing to choose between
जैसे भी हो	By hook or by crook
जोंक की तरह चिपकना / चिपटना / लिपटना	1. Person who cannot be easily shaken off 2. To cling to somebody and not to leave him
जो आकाश पर थूकता है, थूक उसी के मुँह पर आता है	He who blows in the dust fills his own eyes
जो आता है, अपना सिक्का चलाता है	New lords, new laws
जोखिम उठाना	To run the risk, to venture

जोखिम, जान (में डालना)	To risk one's life
जोखिम मोल लेना	To take risk
जोड़-तोड़ करना	1. To exercise ingenuity 2. To manipulate
जोतना, अपनी ही	1. To paddle one's own canoe 2. To work alone
जोर, कलम का	To wield a powerful pen
जोर चलना	To have sway over
जोर चलाना	To use force
जोर पकड़ना	1. To gain intensity 2. To gather momentum
जोश ठंडा पड़ जाना	Fervour to disappear
जोश दिलाना	To excite
जौहर दिखाना	To show one's mettle
ज्यों-त्यों	1. Somehow 2. With great difficulty

झंझट मोल लेना	To invite trouble, to involve oneself in difficulties
झंडा गाड़ना	1. To achieve victory 2. To conquer
झंडा फहराना	1. To come out victoriously 2. To hoist a flag
झंडी दिखाना (हरी)	To give a green signal
झंडे गाड़ देना	To come out with flying colours, To win credit
झंडे तले आना	To come under one banner/ one leader and for one cause
झक चढ़ना	To be crazy, to be obstinate
झक / झख मारना	To do nothing, To engage oneself in some fruitless job
झक सवार होना	To be crazy about/wild about
झगड़ा मोल लेना / खरीदना	To assume the aggressive, To pick up a quarrel

झगड़े की जड़	Apple of discord, Bone of contention
झटका खाना	To get a jolt, To get shock
झटका देना	To give a jolt
झपट्टे में आना	To fall into the clutches of
झमेला खड़ा करना	To create an inbroglio
झलक दिखाना	To show a glimpse
झाँसा देना	To deceive, to dodge
झाड़ू देना / फेरना	To make a clean sweep of everything
झाड़ू फिर जाना	To lose one's all
झूठ का पुतला	A consummate liar
झूठी खुशामद	1. Apple sauce 2. Insincere flattery
झोंकना, भाड़	To engage oneself in a worthless job
झोंक में आकर करना	To act impulsively
झोंटा पकड़कर निकाल देना	To turn out insultingly
झोली फैलाना	1. To receive alms 2. To seek favour
झोली में डालना	To donate. To give away

टंटा खड़ा करना	To make a fuss
टंटा मचाना	To kick up a row
टका-सा जवाब	Curt reply, Flat refusal, To refuse point blank
टका सीधा करना	To achieve one's objective
टके को न पूछना	Not to get attention from anybody An insignificant being
टके-सा मुँह लेकर लौटना	To return with downcast looks
टके सेर पंसेरी बिकना	To sell awfully cheap
टक्कर का होना	To be a match for
टक्कर खाना	To bump, To knock about
टक्कर झेलना	To prove equal to the task
टक्कर लेना	To face the music, To face a rival
टक्कर लेना, पहाड़ से	1. To be up against a giant 2. To face an opponent much superior in strength 3. To fight against heavy odds

टक्करें खाना	1. To be driven from pillar to post 2. To collide against
टक्करें मारना	1. To roam about aimlessly 2. To strive in vain
टट्टी की ओट में शिकार खेलना	1. To act clandestinely 2. To attack from behind a smoke-screen
टट्टी, धोखे की	A camouflage, A smokescreen, Deceptive appearance
टट्टू पार करना	To achieve an objective
टट्टू, भाड़े का	A hireling, A mercenary
टपक पड़ना	To drop suddenly
टर-टर करना	To keep harping on the same point
टल जाना	To blow over
टलना, बात से	To go back on one's word
टस-से-मस न होना	Not to budge an inch, Not to compromise
टाँके उधेड़ना	To undo completely
टाँग अड़ाना	1. To butt in, to interfere 2. To intervene 3. To intrude into another man's sphere 4. To poke one's nose 5. To put an impediment/ obstruction

	6. To put in one's oar
टाँग तले से निकलना	To concede supremacy, To humble oneself before
टाँग तले से निकालना	To bend to one's will
टाँग पसारकर सोना	1. To be at one's ease 2. To be carefree 3. To sleep at leisure
टाँय-टाँय फिस्स होना	1. To come to nothing 2. To end up in smoke 3. To flop
टाट उलटना	To go bankrupt
टिप्पस भिड़ाना/लगाना	1. To find a way out 2. To manipulate
टुकड़े तोड़ना (के)	To sponge on
टुकड़ों पर पलना	To live on leavings
टूक, दो (करना)	1. Crystal clear 2. To break
टूक, दो (जवाब देना)	1. To give a clear-cut refusal 2. A precise and to-the-point answer
टूटना, आस	To lose hope
टूट पड़ना	To attack violently, To fly at, To pounce upon suddenly
टें-टें करना	To indulge in useless talk
टेकना, लाठी	To take rest
टेकना, घुटने	1. To kneel down 2. To surrender
टेकना, माथा	To bow down, to yield

टेक निभाना	1. To carry out one's firm intention 2. To fulfill one's promise
टेढ़ा मामला	Complicated affair/matter
टेढ़ी खीर	A hard nut to crack
टोपी उछालना	1. To humiliate, to insult 2. To put one to public shame
टोपी उतारना	To insult
टोह पाना	To find a clue
टोह रखना	To keep track, to watch over
टोह लगाना	To hint out, to search out
टोह लेना	To find out, to trace

ठंडा करके खाना	1. Act in haste, have nasty taste 2. To draw a line on one's greed 3. To play it cool
ठंडा (ठंढा) करना	To cool, to pacify, to put out
ठंडा पड़ना	To be pacified, To calm down
ठंडा लोहा गरम लोहे को काटता है	1. A soft answer turns away wrath 2. Discretion is the better part of valour
ठंडा होना	1. Dull market (बाजार) 2. To have one's revenge (कलेजा) 3. To pass away (व्यक्ति) 4. To turn cold/frigid/unresponsive
ठगा-सा रह जाना	To be completely lost/non-plussed, To feel cheated
ठट्ठे में उड़ाना	To laugh off

	To pass off jokingly
ठनठन गोपाल होना	To be without a penny
ठाठ बदलना	To alter the appearance
ठिकाने, अक्ल (आना)	To come to one's senses
ठिकाने का आदमी	A dependable person
ठिकाने की बात	A logical utterance, Authentic statement
ठिकाने पहुँचाना	To dispose of, to kill. to send one to one's destination
ठिकाने लगाना	1. To bring to a happy conclusion 2. To kill, to put to death 3. To provide job 4. To show one his due place
ठीक करना	1. To bring one to one's senses 2. To punish 3. To repair 4. To set right
ठीकरा समझना	To treat as of no value
ठुड्डी पकड़ना	To appease
ठेंगा दिखाना	1. To cock a snook at 2. To disappoint 3. To refuse flatly
ठेंगे, हमारे (से)	1. For all I care 2. Not to care two hoots 3. To care a fig
ठेस देना/पहुँचाना	To give a jolt/setback
(मन को आघात लगाना)	To hurt one's feelings
ठोंकना, पीठ	To give a pat on one's back,

	To pat someone on the back
ठोक बजाकर देखना (पीटकर देखना)	1. To check up thoroughly 2. To examine minutely 3. To put person through his paces 4. To test one's qualities in action
ठोकर खाकर सीखना	To learn from one's mistakes
ठोकर खाना	To suffer reverse
ठोकरों पर पड़े रहना	To suffer indignities while being dependent on others
ठोड़ी में हाथ डालना (अनुनय-विनय करना)	To beseech, To entreat, To implore

ड

डंक मारना	To pass a caustic/stinging remark
डंका बजना	To be far-famed, To be renowned
डंका बजाना	1. To gain recognition all over 2. To pronounce publicly
डंके की चोट कहना	To announce openly, To proclaim openly, To tell the world
डंडे का राज	1. Club law 2. Law of jungle
डंडे के जोर से	By physical force, forcibly
डंडे बजाते फिरना	To wander idly about
डंडे बजाना	To while away time in idle pursuits
डंडे से (जादू के)	With magic wand
डकार जाना	To swallow
डकार लेना	To misappropriate
डकार (तक न) लेना	To have no qualms in appropriating another man's due
डटे रहना	Hold one's own

डाँट में रखना	To keep one in check
डाल डाल तुम, मैं पात-पात	1. I am more than a match for you in all respects 2. If you go deep, I can go deeper in the matter
डाल देना	To thrust in
डाल पर रहना (एक)	To be of congenial temperament
डालना, आँखों में आँखें	To look into each other's eyes
डालना, जान जोखिम में	To imperil one's life
डींग मारना/हाँकना	To boast, to brag
डुबकी लगा जाना	To slip away for a long while
डूबते को तिनके का सहारा	A drowning man catches at a straw
डूब मरना (चुल्लू-भर पानी में)	To be too ashamed to show one's face
डेढ़ कौड़ी का	Worthless
डेढ़ चावल की खिचड़ी अलग पकाना	1. To blow one's lone trumpet 2. To paddle one's own canoe 3. To plough a lonely furrow
डेढ़ पसली का	1. Bag of bones 2. Of thin constitution 3. Sickly person
डेढ़ बात करना	To be brief and to the point
डोरे डालना (पर)	1. To allure, to woo someone 2. To set one's cap at 3. To set one's heart on 4. To try to attract someone
डोरी ढीली छोड़ना	1. To give a long rope 2. To give undue freedom 3. To relax discipline

ढंग, अपने (का अकेला)	1. Eccentric 2. Original, unique, unparelleled
ढंग (अपने) पर लाना	1. To bring one round to one's views 2. To make one toe one's line
ढाई दिन की बादशाहत	Short-lived rule
ढाई बजना (चेहरे पर)	To look downcast
ढाक के तीन पात (सदा एक-सा)	To be always in the same predicament
ढिंढोरा पीटना	To blaze abroad, To spread news
ढेर करना	1. To amass 2. To kill
ढेर हो जाना	1. To lie dead 2. To pass away
ढोल की पोल खोलना	1. To call a person's bluff 2. To make one show one's cards 3. To prick the bubble
ढोल बजाना, गले पड़ा	1. To assume an undesired responsibility 2. To hold the baby

तंग आना	1. To be fed up, to be sick of
	2. To be tired
तंग करना	1. To pressurise
	2. To tease
तंग, हाथ (होना)	1. To be hard up
	2. To be short of money
तकदीर का खुलना	To have a sudden turn of fortune
तकदीर का खेल	1. Irony of fate
	2. Wonder wrought by luck
तकदीर का धनी/सिकंदर	An extremely lucky person,
	A lucky guy
तकदीर ठोंकना	To curse one's lot
तकदीर फूट जाना	To change for the worse,
	To fall into adversity
तकदीर लड़ना	To get a favourable chance
तकिया कलाम	An expletive,
	A needless word/phrase used repeatedly
तख्ता उलट जाना	To collapse,
	To turn the tables on

तख्ता उलटना	To overthrow, To topple
तख्ता पलटना	To bring about a coup
तगड़ा असामी	Financially sound client
तगड़ा पड़ना	To prove more than a match, To prove stronger
तड़ी देना	To brag, To get on one's high horse
तड़ी मारना	To give oneself airs, To try to be vainglorious
तन-बदन में आग लगना	To get one's goat
तन-मन से सेवा करना	To serve with all physical and mental resources, To serve with singleminded devotion
तन-मन मारना	To restrain desires
तबियत लगना	To be attached to, To feel at home, To take pleasure in
तमाम करना/ होना (काम)	To be put to death, To die, to be finished
तमाशा करना	To act a part
तमाशा खड़ा करना	To create a scene
तमाशा देखना	1. To sit on the fence 2. To sit on the rail
तरंग में आना	To be in a pleasant mood, To be in one's element
तरंग में होना	To be in light mood, To be on top of the world

तरकीब निकालना/लगाना/लड़ाना	To devise a strategy
तरफ देखना, अपनी	To consider one's own position
तरस आना/खाना	To be moved to pity, To pity, to take pity on
तरसाना, दाने-दाने को	To drive one to the brink of starvation, To grudge the very means of existence
तलवार की धार	Most hazardous path, To skate on thin ice
तलवार के घाट उतारना	To kill, to put to the sword
तलवारें, दो (एक म्यान में)	Two of a trade seldom agree Two swords cannot be contained in one sheath
तलवे चाटना	1. To fawn upon, to flatter 2. To indulge in abject flattery
तलवे छलनी होना	1. To have a tiring and arduous journey 2. To run from pillar to post
तलवे धो-धोकर पीना	1. To be servile 2. To perform humiliating services 3. To be highly grateful to someone who did some great favour
तलवे न लगना	Not to rest
तलवों में आग लगना	1. To be furiously angry 2. To be extremely jealous
तवा, उलटा	A person of jet-black complexion

तवा सिर से बाँधना	To prepare to defend oneself
तवे की बूँद	1. A flash in the pan 2. Something of short duration
तवे-सा मुँह	1. Blackamoor 2. Disgraced
तशरीफ लाना	To grace the occasion with one's presence
तशरीफ ले जाना	To depart
तह तक पहुँचना	To get to the bottom of
तहलका मचाना	To create a sensation
ताँता बँधना/लगना	1. Endless stream of visitors 2. To continue non-stop
ताँता, विचारों का	1. Current of thoughts 2. Flow of ideas
ताऊ, बछिया के	Stupid person, Simpleton, a born fool
ताक[१] पर धरना	To shelve
ताक पर रख देना	1. Not to make use of 2. To put aside 3. To put on the shelf
ताक[२] पर होना	To become ineffective, To be left on the shelf
ताक में रखना	To keep watch over
ताक में रहना	To be on the lookout for an opportunity
ताक लगाना	To lie in wait for
तान तोड़ना	1. To make a mess of a thing 2. To try to be overbearing

तान, लंबी (कर सोना)	To enjoy a sound slumber after accomplishing something great
ताब, आब न देखना	To be unmindful of reputation/ honour
तार टूटना	To break the continuity/ sequence
तार-तार करना	To reduce to shreds
तार-तार होना	To be reduced to smithereens
तार बाँधना	To continue without interruption
तारे गिनना	To keep awake the whole night, To pass the night restlessly
तारीफ के पुल बाँधना	To praise to the skies
तारे टूटना	The onset of misfortune
तारे तोड़ लाना	To perform the impossible/a miracle
तारे दिखाई देना	1. To be utterly confused 2. To see stars fleeting before one's eyes
ताल-मेल बैठाना	To coordinate
ताला-कुंजी हाथ में होना	To be in absolute possession
ताली पिट जाना	To get hooted down on the stage
ताली पिटना	To become a laughing stock
ताली नहीं बजती, एक हाथ से	It takes two to make a quarrel
ताव आना/खाना	To burst into a fit of anger, To be infuriated

ताव, मूँछों पर (देना)	1. To be safe and secure 2. To rest on one's laurels 3. To twirl one's moustaches in bravado
ताव में आना	To be enraged
ताव में होना	To be in high spirits
तिड़ी हो जाना	To flee, To show a clean pair of heels, To slip away
तिनका तोड़ना	To break off connections, to sever relations
तिनका दाँतों में पकड़ना	To confess inferiority
तिनका (तकमी) न तोड़ना	Not to do any work
तिनके का पहाड़ बनाना	To make a mountain of a mole hill
तिनके का सहारा (डूबते को)	A drowning man catches at a straw
तिनके की ओट पहाड़	A large issue lurking behind a seemingly trivial question
तिलक लगाने से कोई संत नहीं हो जाता	All are not saints that go to the church
तिल का ताड़ बनाना	1. To make a mountain of a mole hill 2. To exaggerate beyond measure
तिल-तिल करके मरना	To die by inches
तिल-भर का अंतर	Within an ace of
तिल-भर जगह न होना	To be packed to capacity
तिलों में तेल नहीं (इन)	To yield nothing worthwhile

तीतर, आधा (आधा बटेर)	Incongruous, Neither fish nor fowl
तीन का टट्टू तेरह की जीन	A penny plain and two pence coloured
तीन-छह का रिश्ता	Sworn rivals To be perpetually opposed to each other
तीन-तेरह होना	To be scattered
तीन-पाँच करना	To dilly-dally, to quarrel, to squabble, To talk rot
तीन में-न तेरह में	1. Detached in every way 2. Not to be in any reckoning 3. A small fry
तीन-लोक से न्यारा/न्यारी	1. Of unique type 2. To be peerless 3. Without parallel
तीर कमान से निकल जाना	1. The die is cast 2. The course has been irrevocably decided
तीर-तुक्का जमाना	To make uninformed remarks, To make wild guess
तीर निशाने पर मारना	To hit the mark
तीर मारना	To achieve something
तीस-मार खाँ	Braggart Sham hero
तुक भिड़ाना	To make conjectures
तुक-में-तुक मिलाना	To sing in the same strain
तू-तड़ाक	1. Boorish language

	2. Uncouth in manners
तू-तड़ाक करना	To behave boorishly
तूती की आवाज (नक्करखाने में)	A cry in wilderness
तूती बोलना	1. To enjoy an unchallengeable position 2. To enjoy good repute 3.To have an unquestionable influence
तू-तू, मैं-मैं	An altercation
तूफान उठाना	To raise a commotion, To unleash a storm
तूल देना	To carry too far To overstress a point
तूल पकड़ना	To take a serious turn, To take a violent turn, To go too far
तेल, न नौ मन (होय), न राधा नाचे	When the sky falls, we shall catch larks
तेल निकालना	1. To exact back-breaking work (out of someone) 2. To make one toil beyond one's capacity
तेली का काम तमोली से नहीं होता	Every cobbler should stick to his last
तेली का बैल	1. Toiling wretch 2. A drudging creature
तेवर चढ़ाना	To frown
तेवर बदलना	1. To assume an angry look 2. To change one's expression

	3. To raise eye-brows as sign of anger
तैश खाना (उत्तेजित होना)	To go into a huff
तैश में आना	To fly into a rage
तोड़ना, कमर	1. To break the back of
	2. To work very hard
	3. To render ineffective
तोड़ना, कलम	1. To write exceptionally well
	2. To write the final word
तोड़ना, दम	To breathe one's last
तोड़ना, हौसला	To discourage, to dishearten
तोता उड़ जाना, हाथों से	1. To be much perplexed,
	2. To be non-plussed
तोते की तरह आँखें फेर लेना	1. To assume cool indifference
	2. To be faithless
	3. To cut someone dead
	4. To refuse to recognize
तोते की तरह रटना	1. To continue to harp on the same note
	2. To learn by rote
	3. To repeat unintelligently
तोते पालना	1. To get addicted to something
	2. To nurse a sore
त्यौरी चढ़ना	1. Assuming an angry look
	2. To knit one's brows

थ

थाली का बैंगन	Fickle-minded person
थाली बजाना	To rejoice at the birth of a son
थाली में घी इधर या उधर	1. As broad as it is long 2. One way or the other would bring about the same result
थाह लगाना	To assess the depth of
थिगली, आसमान में (लगाना)	To achieve something impossible
थूक कर चाटना	1. To break one's own promise 2. To go back on one's own word 3. To run away from one's own guns 4. To eat one's word
थू-थू होना	To be condemned/scorned
थैली के चट्टे-बट्टे, एक ही	Chips of the same block
थैली खोलना	To disburse money
थोथी बातें	Empty talks
थोबड़ा फुलाना (रूठना)	To be sulky

दखल देना (में)	To interfere, To poke one's nose
दखल पाना	To get possession, To have access
दक्षिण होना	To be favourably disposed
दफा करना	To ward off
दबी जबान से	With subdued voice, To say in a hushed manner
दबे पैरों से चलना	To move stealthily To walk without being noticed
दम, नाक में (आना)	To be fed up, To be very distressed
दम, नाकों (करना)	To get on one's nerves, To pester beyond limit
दम तोड़ना	To kick the bucket
दम भरना	1. To repose full confidence 2. To boast, to profess
दम मारना	1. To puff at a cigarette etc. 2. To rest a while
दम लेना	To take rest

दम सूखना	To be mortally scared, To be terrified beyond measure
दरखास्त करना	To apply, to move, to request
दर-दर की खाक छानना	To knock about from pillar to post
दरवाजा बंद करना	To sever all relations, To shut the door on someone
दरवाजे की मिट्टी खोद डालना	To visit someone too frequently
दरार पड़ना	A rift to be created
दरिया को कूजे में बंद करना	To be concise in speech
दर्द आना	To feel compassion/pity
दर्द का मारा	A sufferer
दवा, किसी मर्ज की (न होना)	To be good for nothing
दस्तरखान की बिल्ली	Uninvited guest
दहलीज का कुत्ता	Parasite
दहलीज न झाँकना	To cease to visit
दहशत पैदा करना, दिल में	To strike terror into the hearts
दही को हर कोई सराहता है, अपने	Every potter praises his own pot
दाँत काटी रोटी होनी	To be chummy/close friends
दाँत किरकिरे होना	To suffer a setback
दाँत खट्टे करना	1. To force the enemy into a tight corner 2. To make one lick the dust
दाँत खट्टे होना	1. To kiss the dust 2. To fall 3. To yield
दाँत तोड़ना	To render powerless/toothless
दाँत दिखाना	To show meekness

दाँत निकालना	To express helplessness
दाँत से पैसा/दमड़ी पकड़ना	To be very stingy
दाँतों तले उँगली दबाना	To be aghast/amazed/ wonderstruck
दाँतों में तिनका दबाना	1. To express unconditional surrender 2. To yield unconditionally
दाँतों में तिनका लेना	To show submissiveness in the face of displeasure
दाँव पर चढ़ना	To be caught with chaff, To come in one's grip
दाँव पर रखना	To wager
दाँव पर लगाना	To stake
दाँव फेंकना	To throw the dice
दाँव में आना	To walk into one's trap
दाई से पेट छिपाना	To conceal something from a person who knows/or can know easily
दाएँ-बाएँ करना	1. To conceal 2. To dissemble
दाग लगाना	To defame
दाढ़ी नोच लेना	To dishonour an elderly person
दान, तुरंत (महाकल्याण)	He gives thrice who gives in a trice
दाना-पानी उठना	To be forced to move away
दाना-पानी छोड़ना	To fast
दाने-दाने को तरसना/ मुहताज हो जाना	To be in abject penury, To be on the verge of starvation

दाम सँवारे सारे काम	Money makes the mare go
दाम, चाम के (चलाना)	To act arbitrarily to gratify a whim
दामन, चोली (का नाता)/ (का साथ)	1. Intimate connection 2. To be hand in glove with
दामन छुड़ाना	To get rid of, to free oneself from
दामन पकड़ना/थामना	To come under the protection/ shelter of
दामन फैलाना	To beg/beseech, to supplicate
दामन में दाग होना	1. A blot on one's escutcheon 2. A broken feather in one's wing
दामन से लगाना	To depend upon
दाल गलना	1. To be effective 2. To sell one's wares 3. To take advantage by tricks
दाल, जूतियों में (बँटना)	1. Parties to come to blows 2. To be at loggerheads
दाल दलिया करना	1. To conclude (better or worse) 2. To decide this way or that way
दाल न गलना	To cut no ice
दाल-भात में मूसलचंद	An unwanted person, An unwelcome presence
दाल में कुछ काला होना	1. To see something fishy 2. To smell a rat 3. To suspect foul play
दावत करना/देना	To invite

दाहिना हाथ होना	To be the right hand man, A dependable and most trusted associate
दिन काटना	To pass one's days willy-nilly
दिन दो का मेहमान	One whose days are numbered
दिन को / में तारे दिखना	1. To be beaten severely 2. To be so engrossed in mental work as to become oblivious of one's surroundings
दिन को रात कहना	To reverse the truth
दिन चढ़ना	1. To be in the family way 2. The day to advance
दिन चार की चाँदनी	1. Nine days wonder 2. Transitory affluence
दिन दूना-रात चौगुना	By leaps and bounds
दिन पूरे करना	To drag on one's days, To mark time
दिन फिरना	Dame luck to smile on someone, Time to take a favourable turn
दिन भारी होना	To be in dire straits
दिन लद जाना	Hey days to be past
दिनों का फेर	1. Change in fortunes (usually for the worse) 2. Dark days 3. Time to take a turn for the worse or the better
दिमाग का पुरजा ढीला होना	To have a screw loose
दिमाग खाना/चाटना	To bore, To talk too much for nothing,

	To tax other's brain
दिमाग गरम होना	To lose one's temper
दिमाग चढ़ना	To be arrogant, to get inflated
दिमाग लड़ाना	To ruminate, To tax one's brain
दिमाग सातवें आसमान पर होना	To be swollen-headed, To be very conceited, To grow too big for one's boots
दिल आना	To take a fancy to
दिल का बादशाह होना	To be a king at heart
दिल की कली खिलना	To be beside oneself with joy, To feel jubilant
दिल की दिल में रह जाना	One's longing to remain unfulfilled
दिल के फफोले फोड़ना	1. To reopen (one's) old sores 2. To unburden one's mind
दिल खट्टा होना	To feel sore
दिल तोड़ना	To break one's heart
दिल पक जाना	To be totally fed up
दिल पकड़े फिरना	To wear one's heart on one's sleeve
दिल भर आना	To be moved
दिल मसोसकर रह जाना	To bear silently, To feel frustated in one's heart
दिल में फफोले पड़ना	To suffer mental agony
दिल हलका करना	To unburden oneself
दिलो-जान से	1. From the bottom of one's heart 2. Heart and soul 3. Whole-heartedly

	4. With all one's heart
दिल्लगी उड़ाना/में उड़ाना	1. To laugh away, to laugh off (a remark) 2. To make fun of
दीमक लग जाना	1. To be termite-infested 2. To become useless
दीये तले अँधेरा	Nearer the church, farther from God
दीवार के भी कान होते हैं	Even walls have ears, Hedges have eyes
दीवार (दिवाल) ढह जाना	Barriers to be razed
दुकान, ऊँची (फीके पकवान)	Great boast, small roast, Much cry, little wool
दुःख आता है पहाड़/घुड़दौड़-सा	Sorrow is soon enough when it comes
दुखती रग छेड़ना	To touch one on the raw, To touch one's sore spot
दुनिया की हवा लगना	To acquire worldly wiles
दुनिया देखना	To gather wide and varied experience
दुनिया से उठ जाना	To give up the ghost, To pass away
दुम दबाकर भागना	To run away with one's tail between one's legs, To show a clean pair of heels
दुम दबा जाना	To be scared away
दुम हिलाते फिरना	To hang on
दुम हिलाना	1. To beg 2. To fawn/flatter

दुश्मनी मोल लेना	To invite hostility
दूज का चाँद	1. An infrequent visitor 2. One who is seen once in a blue moon 3. One whose visits have become few and far between
दूध-का-दूध और पानी-का-पानी	Sifting of just from unjust
दूध का धोया/धुला	A man of unimpeachable character,
दूध की मक्खी	1. An unwanted person 2. Insignificant being 3. Something that spoils good things
दूध-को-दूध और पानी-को-पानी कहना	1. To be an impartial judge 2. To call a spade a spade 3. To hold the scales even
दूध देना पर मेंगनी डालकर	1. Grace lies not in giving the gift but in the manner in which it is given 2. To do a kind thing in a very brusque and ungracious manner
दूध लजाना, माँ का	To shame one's family's honour
दूधों नहाना पूतों फलना	To flourish in wealth and progeny, May you prosper in cattle and children!
दून की हाँकना	To indulge in tall talk
दूर की कौड़ी	1. A far-sighted view

	2. To propose something fantastic
दूर की न सोचना	1. To take a short-sighted view 2. To live in the present only
दूर की हाँकना	To beat the dutch To say something incredible
दूर से नमस्कार/ सलाम करना	To give wide berth to, To keep at an arm's length
दृष्टि फेरना	To withdraw one's favours
दृष्टि बचाना	To avoid meeting
दृष्टि रखना	To keep under observation
देखते रह जाना	To hold one's breath
देखा-अनदेखा करना	1. To affect not to see 2. To blink the fact 3. To turn one's blind eye to
देर आयद दुरुस्त आयद	Better late than never
देर-दार	Delay
दो की चार सुनाना	To pay back in full measure
दो कौड़ी का	Worthless
दो-चार दिन का मेहमान	At death's door, To be on death-bed
दो-टूक जवाब	To reply categorically
दो-दो बातें करना	To exchange views unreservedly
दो-दो हाथ करना/होना	1. To have it out 2. To measure swords with
दो नावों पर पैर रखना	1. No man can serve two masters 2. To fall between two stools 3. To ride two horses at a time

दोनों हाथ में लड्डू होना	To have the best of both the worlds
दोनों हाथों से लुटाना	To burn the candle at both the ends
दो पाटों के बीच पिसना	To be pounded between mortar and pestle
दोष, समरथ को नहीं (गुसाईं)	The king does no wrong, Those in power, commit no sin
दोस्ती का दम भरना	To profess friendship
दौड़-धूप	1. Hectic activity 2. Running about 3. Strenuous effort
दौड़-धूप करना	To put in a lot of effort

ध

धक्का खाना/देना	1. To give a push/support 2. To receive a setback 3. To suffer misfortune/loss
धक्के खाना	To run from pillar to post without achieving the objective
धज्जियाँ उड़ा देना	1. To give short shrift to 2. To knock the bottom out of 3. To make short work of 4. To tear (arguments etc.) into shreds
धज्जियाँ उड़ना	To be reduced to shreds
धड़े बँधना	Factions to come into being within a larger group/party
धता बताना	1. To drive one away 2. To have no more to do with 3. To put someone off
धन की अपेक्षा सुनाम अच्छा	Good name is better than riches
धन देता है तो छप्पर फाड़कर देता है	It never rains but it pours

धनी, कलम	One who wields an effective pen
धनी-धोरी	Person of influence
धनी-वर्ग	Upper crust
धनी, बात का	One who is true to one's word
धरती पर पैर न रखना	To fly high
धर दबोचना	1. To pin down 2. To pounce upon and overpower
धरा रह जाना	To come to naught
धरे रहना	1. To hoard 2. To keep in reserve stock
धर्म कमाना / करना	To give alms, To obtain fruits of virtuous life
धाक जमाना / बँधना	To dominate, To hold sway
धाक बैठना / बैठाना	To command a dominating position, To establish overwhelming influence
धाकड़ होना	To be dashing
धार मारना	To treat with contempt
धावा मारना / बोलना	To cover a long distance, To launch a raid, To make a forced march
धुआँधार भाषण	Fiery speech
धुआँधार वर्षा	Torrential rain
धुन का पक्का होना	To be persevering
धुन सवार होना	1. To be driven by an urge

	2. To be obsessed
	3. To have a bee in one's bonnet
धूंनी-पानी का संजोग	Close attachment
धूनी रमाना / लगाना	1. To become ascetic
	2. To pursue a goal till it is achieved
धूप में बाल सफेद करना	To grow grey without gaining any wisdom
धूम मचाना	To gain recognition all over
धूल उड़ना	To be disgraced
धूल की रस्सी बँटना	To try to perform something impossible
धूल चटाना	To make someone lick the dust
धूल चाटना	1. To bite the dust
	2. To make entreaties
	3. To put up with insult
	4. To submit to humiliation
धूल छानना	To toil hard fruitlessly
धूल झोंकना	To throw dust in the eyes of
धूल, पैरों की	Insignificant person
धूल फाँकना	To roam about aimlessly
धूल में मिलना / मिलाना	To be ruined,
	To ruin
धूल में लट्ठ मारना	To make a vain bid,
	To strike in vain
धूल समझना	To care a fig for
धोकर, हाथ (पड़ना)	To pursue with a vengeance
धोखे की टट्टी	A concealed danger,

	Trojan horse
धोखे की टट्टी खड़ी करना	To put up a smokescreen
धोती ढीली होना	To lose all courage
धोबी का कुत्ता घर का न घाट का	Between two stools, one cometh to the ground
धोवन, पैर का (होना)	To be far below the mark
	To be not fit to hold a candle to

न

नंगा करना	To disgrace, To expose
नंगा नाच करना	To conduct disgracefully
नई राह दिखाना	To blaze a trail
नकेल किसी के हाथ में होना	To be in leading strings
नकेल हाथ में होना	1. To dominate completely 2. To lead by the nose
नक्कारखाने में तूती की आवाज	A cry in the wilderness
नक्कारे की चोट	Openly, publicly
नक्कू बनना	Not conforming to a generally accepted pattern of thought or action, To draw all eyes to oneself by breaking a tradition
नक्शा बैठाना	To establish authority
नक्शा जमाना	To create an impression
नक्शे दिखाना	To put on airs
नखरा दिखाना	To be under false pretences, To give oneself airs
न खाये न खाने दे	A dog-in-the manger

नजर खाना	To be afflicted by an evil eye
नजर पर चढ़ना	To develop liking for, To take a fancy for
नजर बचाना	To avoid meeting
नजर बदल लेना	To change one's stance
नजर मिलाना	To look straight into one's eyes
नजर रखना	To keep a watch, To supervise
नजर लगना	To fall a prey to an evil eye
नजर लगाना	To cast an evil eye
नजर से गिरना	To fall in esteem
नजरों में चढ़ना	1. To be in the good books of 2. To be in one's good graces
नजरों में भरना	To devour with the eyes
नजरों में समाना	To be always in the mind
नजरों में होना	To be in one's mind
नजला गिरना	Displeasure to fall
न तीतर न बटेर	Neither hawk nor buzzard
नथने फुलाना	To be infuriated
नथ बढ़ाना	To become a widow
नदी नाव संयोग	Chance meeting
नफा-नुकसान समझना	To know which side one's bread is buttered
नब्ज पकड़ना	To get at one's weak point
नब्ज पहचानना	To know someone out and out
नमक अदा करना	To discharge one's obligations To prove one's loyalty
नमक, कटे जले पर (छिड़कना)	To add insult to injury, To rub salt in someone's wounds

नमक खाना	To subsist on one's patronage
नमक, दाल में (खाना)	To charge most reasonable profit
नमक-मिर्च लगाना	1. To give a false colour to 2. To narrate with a pinch of salt
नमक हक अदा करना (का)	To be true to one's salt
नमक हलाल	Loyal to one's master
नमस्कार, दूर से (करना)	To keep one at an arm's length
नया-नया नौकर बढ़िया काम करता है	A new broom sweeps clean
नया नौ दिन पुराना सौ दिन	1. New brands are not better than old ones 2. The new fades and the old endures
नये गुल खिलाना	1. To start new mischief 2. To venture into new exploits
नरक का कीड़ा	A despicable creature
नरक हो जाना	To become hellish, To become unbearably miserable
नरम पड़ जाना	To mellow, To tone down
नरमी दिखाना	To show leniency
नशा उतरना / हिरन होना	To become sober, To sober up in an instant
नस दबना	To be under one's thumb
नस-नस फड़क उठना	1. To be thrilled 2. To get inspired to do a heroic deed
नस-नस में होना	To be in the blood

नहले पर दहला मारना/लगाना	1. To be more than a match for 2. To be one up on someone
नाक ऊँची होना	To acquire added status, To add a new feather to one's cap
नाक कटना	1. To have one's fair name tarnished 2. To lose face
नाक काटना	1. To dishonour 2. To inflict humiliation
नाक का बाल	A close associate with whom all secrets are shared
नाक की सीध में	As the crow flies, In a straight line
नाक घिसना	To make servile entreaties
नाक चढ़ाना (भौं)	1. To show anger/annoyance/ sign of disapproval to
नाक तक पानी आना	To come to the end of one's tether, To reach the limit of one's patience
नाक तोड़ना	1.To affront 2. To show unwillingness
नाक पर गुस्सा होना	To be short-tempered
नाक पर मक्खी न बैठने देना	1. To be conceited 2. To be quick to take offence 3. To let none get an upper hand

	4. To quarrel even with one's own shadow
नाक में दम करना/नाकों दम करना	1. To get on one's nerves
	2. To harass
	3. To make it too hot for
नाक रखना	To maintain one's honour,
	To save one's face
नाक रगड़वाना	To make one eat the humble pie
नाखून गड़ाना	To go deep into a matter
नाग खिलाना	1. To endanger one's life
	2. To play with fire
नाच उठना	To dance with joy
नाच नचाना	To harass
	To make one dance on one's finger tips
नाज उठाना	To bear with the alluring gestures of
नाज नखरे न मिलना	To be insufferably high brow
नाटक करना / रचना	To put up an unreal show
नानी के आगे ननिहाल की बातें	1. Explaining to Noah the story of the deluge
	2. Old birds are not to be caught by chaff
नानी मरना	To be in a sad predicament
नानी याद आना	To fall into too serious a trouble
नाम उछालना	To bring disgrace to one's fair name
नाम उजागर करना	1. To tarnish the image of

	2. To win laurels
नाम उठ जाना	To be left with no one to take one's name
नाम कमाना	1. To make one's mark 2. To win oneself a name
नाम कर जाना	To leave a good name behind
नाम करना	To establish a good name
नाम की माला जपना	To chant the praises of
नाम चमकना	1. Name stands high 2. To leave one's mark
नाम डुबोना	To tarnish the fair name of
नाम धरना	To blame
नाम निकलना	To become well known
नाम निशान बाकी न रखना	To erase even the name of
नाम निशान मिट जाना	To have no trace left behind
नाम पड़ना	To be debited
नाम बड़े और दर्शन थोड़े	1. Great boast, little roast 2. Much cry, little wool
नाम रखना	1. To name 2. To save one's honour
नाम रोशन होना	To become celebrated
नाम लगना	To be charged with
नाम लिखना	To hold responsible
नाल गड़ी/गड़ा होना	To have a hereditary claim to a place
नाव, कागज की	A house of cards, A transitory thing
नावों, दो (पर पैर चलाना/रखना)	1. To embark on two contradictory courses

	2. To serve two masters
निगाह चुराना	Not being able to look one in the face
निगाह पर चढ़ना	To rise in the estimation
निगाह रखना (में)	1. To keep in one's mind 2. To keep watch on
निगाहें मिलाना	To exchange glances
निर्धनता कलह की जड़ है	Poverty breeds strife
निन्यानवे के चक्कर (फेर) में पड़ना/होना	1. Intent on amassing wealth 2. To be involved in difficulties 3. To be obsessed by a desire to augment one's savings
निपोरना / निपोड़ना दाँत	1. To cut a sorry figure 2. Unable to reply
निबाह करना	To pass time, To pull on
निशाना मारना	To hit the target
निशाना लगना	To hit exactly
निहाई की चोरी और सुई का दान	Steal a goose and give giblets in alms
नींद हराम होना	To be disturbed in sleep, To be restless, To get no sleep, To pass sleepless nights
नीचा खाना	To suffer a reverse
नीचा दिखाना	1. To bring a person to his knees 2. To humiliate somebody 3. To make one bite the dust

नीचा पड़ना	To be subdued
नीची निगाह से देखना	To look down upon
नीची, निगाह (रखना)	To keep the eyes downcast
नीचे गिराना	To humble someone or oneself
नीम न मीठी होय सींचों गुड़ घी से	Crows are never the whiter for washing
नीम हकीम खतरा-ए-जान	1. A little knowledge is a dangerous thing 2. A quack endangers life
नीयत का साफ	A man of integrity
नीयत न भरना	Not to feel satisfied
नीयत भर जाना	To feel satisfied
नीयत में फर्क आना	To be swayed by malafide intentions
नीर-क्षीर विवेक	Discrimination between right and wrong
नीला करना	To beat black and blue
नीला-पीला होना	To be enraged To be infuriated
नुक्ता-चीनी करना	To carp, To criticise, To find fault
नेकी कर दरिया में डाल	Do good turn and forget it
नोक-झोंक करना	To altercate with, To have words with
नोक-झोंक होना	To enter into an altercation, To have a wordy duel with
नौकरी बजाना	To dance attendance on
नौ दो ग्यारह हो जाना	1. To make good one's escape

	2. To show a clean pair of one's heels,
	3. To take to one's heels
नौ निध बारह सिद्ध होना	To have all that the heart can aspire for
नौबत आना/पहुँचना	1. Things to come to such a pass
	2. Time to be ripe for certain actions to be taken
	3. To reach an impasse
नौबत बजना	Beating of drums

पंख निकलना	To give oneself airs To take risks
पंख लगना	1. To adopt risky ways 2. To move very fast
पंख लगाकर उड़ना	To assume an arrogant or superior attitude
पंगत से बाहर करना	To declare out of caste, To excommunicate, To ostracize
पंगु हो जाना	To be crippled, To become totally helpless
पंजा, छक्का	1. Gambling 2. Trickery
पंजे जमाना	To establish oneself
पंजे फैलाना	1. To attempt to lay hands on 2. To extend one's control
पंजे में आना	1. To come under one's control 2. To fall into the clutches of
पंजे लड़ाना	A trial of strength
पंडिताई छाँटना	To make a parade of one's erudition

पंथ, एक (दो काज)	To kill two birds with one stone
पंथ दिखाना	To guide, To show path
पंथ देखना	To wait eagerly
पकड़ ढीली करना	To loosen one's hold
पकड़-धकड़	General arrest
पकड़ में आना	To come under one's grip
पकना, कलेजा (संताप होना)	To be tormented
पकना, कान	To be fed up
पकाना, बाल	1. To gain experience 2. To grow grey
पक्का करना	1. To confirm 2. To make sure
पक्का, दिल (करना)	To make up one's mind
पक्का, बात (का)	True to one's word
पग उठाना	To venture
पग धरना/फूँक-फूँककर	To exercise utmost caution
पगड़ी उछालना/उतारना	1. To defame, to disgrace, to dishonour 2. To insult 3. To make fun of
पगड़ी, पैरों पर (रखना)	To beg for mercy, To beg most submissively
पगड़ी बदलना	To make friends
पच मरना	1. To toil hard 2. To work hard (to death)
पचड़ा खड़ा करना	To create a fuss
पचड़े में पड़ना	To get embroiled
पचती, बुरी कमाई (नहीं)	Ill got, ill spent

पचना/पचती, पेट में कोई बात नहीं	Unable to keep a secret
पचाना, सारा पैसा	To embezzle the entire money
पच्ची, माथा (करना)	To tax one's brain
पटकना, हाथ-पैर	1. To be extremely restless 2. To leave no stone unturned
पटना, मामला	To settle the matter
पटना, सौदा	To strike a bargain
पटना, हिसाब	To settle the accounts
पटरा कर देना	To ruin completely
पटरा बैठ जाना	To go to dogs
पटरी खाना/बैठना	To get on well, To have harmonious relations
पटरी नहीं बैठना	Not to see eye to eye with each other
पट्टी पढ़ाना	1. To misguide 2. To teach a lesson to 3. To tutor
पट्टी बाँधना (आँखों पर)	To overlook, To take no cognizance of
पड़ता खाना	To suit/fit
पड़ता निकालना	To calculate the cost
पड़ता फैलाना	To distribute an aggregate amount (charge) among those who must pay
पड़ती है, जिस पर वही जानता है	It is only the wearer who knows where the shoe pinches
पड़ना, अक्ल पर पत्थर	Unable to distinguish between right and wrong
पड़ना, अपनी-अपनी	To see only the self-interest

पड़ना, गले	To be thrust upon To be tied round one's neck
पड़ना, झमेलों में	To get involved in complications
पड़ना, पल्ले	To fall to one's lot
पड़ना, सिर	To be thrust upon
पत उतारना	To destroy the reputation To disgrace, to dishonour
पता देना	To give the clue
पता नहीं कब दादा मरें कब बैल मिले	To wait anxiously for one's share in one's ancestral property
पता रखना	To keep oneself posted with the necessary information
पता लगाना, अता—	To run for a clue, to discover
पते की बात कहना (गुत्थी सुलझाना)	1. To be accurate 2. To disclose something secret 3. To hit the mark, to hit the right nail on the head 4. To make a remarkable utterance 5. To solve the puzzle 6. To speak with meticulous exactness
पत्तल (एक) में खाना	To develop intimate relationship
पत्तल में खाना उसी में छेद करना, जिस	To bite the hand that feeds one
पत्ता कटना/कट जाना	To be sacked from one's job
पत्ता खड़कना	Rustling of a dry leaf

पत्ता तक न हिलना	Everything stands still, Not a leaf rustles
पत्ते चाटना	To be in a miserable state
पत्ते लगाना	To stack the cards
पत्थर का कलेजा/दिल	A ruthless heart
पत्थर की छाती	Unwavering will
पत्थर की लकीर	Unalterable opinion
पत्थर छाती पर रखना	To resolve not to move
पत्थर पड़ना, अक्ल पर	To lose one's wits
पत्थर पर दूब जमना	A phenomenon impossible to occur
पत्थर पसीजना	1. The improbable to occur 2. Stony heart is impressed
पत्थर रखकर, छाती पर	With a heavy heart
पत्थर होना	1. To be turned into a stone 2. To become motionless
पर कटना	To be made powerless/toothless
पर कतरना	1. To clip the wings of 2. To cut the claws of
पर जमना	To gain freedom of action
पर निकलना	1. To be free 2. To start giving oneself airs
परदा उठना/उठाना	To be revealed, To expose, to reveal, to unveil
परदा करना	1. To be secretive 2. To observe veil
परदा डालना	To cover up
परदा पड़ना, आँख पर	To be blinded
परदा पड़ना, बुद्धि पर	To lose all senses,

	Unable to distinguish between right and wrong
परदे के पीछे रहना	To work behind the curtain
परदे में रखना	Not to leak, To keep under a veil
पराई आग में हाथ सेंकना	1. To fish in troubled waters 2. To take advantage of a confusion concerning others
पराया, अपना (समझना)	To have sense of discrimination
पराया न समझना	Not to treat as alien
पराया मुँह ताकना	To look to others for help
पलंग तोड़ना	To idle away time
पलक झपकते	In the twinkling of an eye
पलक पसीजना	To be moved by compassion
पलक बिछाना (पलक पाँवड़े)	To extend a respectful/red carpet welcome
पलक लगना	To have a short nap
पलक न मारना	Not to bat an eyelid
पलक से पलक न लगना	To have no sleep at all
पलकें मूँदना	To die
पलकों पर लेना	To show all honour
पलकों से (तिनके) चुनना	To show extreme respect
पलटन-की-पलटन	A big force, A large army
पलटन खड़ी करना	To beget a large number of children
पलटा खाना	To suffer a reverse
पलड़ा ऊँचा होना	To have an upper hand

पलड़ा नीचा होना	To be in a disadvantageous position
पलड़ा भारी होना	To be in a stronger position
पलड़ा हलका होना	1. To be at a discount 2. To turn the scales
पलड़े में रखकर देखना	To weigh dispossionately
पल में तोला-पल में माशा	To blow hot and cold, To play fast and loose, Tongue to be a double-edged sword
पलस्तर ढीला करना	To give a sound beating
पलस्तर बिगड़ना	To be wearied out of countenance
पलीता लगाना	To touch off a fight
पलेथन निकालना	To beat mercilessly
पलेथन लगाना	To praise sky-high
पल्ला छुड़ाना	To get rid of
पल्ला झाड़ना	To pay off all that one has
पल्ला दबना	To be under the thumb of
पल्ला पकड़ना	1. To be under protection of 2. To marry 3. To turn to someone for support
पल्ला पसारना	1. To beg of 2. To supplicate for favour
पल्ला भारी होना	The odds are in his favour
पल्ले पड़ना	To force oneself upon someone
पल्ले बँधना	To be wedded
पल्ले बाँधना	1. To keep in mind

	2. To marry off to someone
पल्ले से बाँधना	1. To marry off
	2. To thrust on
पल्ले होना	To possess
पवाड़ा (पँवाड़ा) खड़ा करना	To kick up a row
पसली ढीली करना	To give severe beating
पसली फड़कना	To be thrilled
पसीना छूट जाना	To have cold feet,
	To perspire profusely out of nervousness
पसीना बहाना	To toil hard
पसीने की कमाई	Hard-earned money
पसीने-पसीने हो जाना	1. To be alarmed
	2. To feel utter shame
	3. To perspire from head to toe
पस्त करना	1. To defeat
	2. To tire one out
पस्त होना	To be wearied out
पस्त, हौसला	Dejected,
	Demoralised,
	To lose heart
पहचानना, नस-नस	To know one thoroughly
पहलू गरम करना	To sit close,
	To sit in a compromising pose
पहलू बचाना	To avoid clash/difficulties
पहलू में रहना	To be in close proximity
पहले आत्मा फिर परमात्मा	Charity begins at home,
	Self before service
पहले तोलो, फिर बोलो	Think before you speak

पहले मारे सो मीर	Well begun is half done
पहले लात पीछे बात	More kicks than half pence
पहाड़ उठाना	To perform an uphill task
पहाड़, खोदा, निकली चुहिया	Mountain was in labour and the mouse was produced, Much ado about nothing, Much cry, little wool
पहाड़ टूटना	A bolt from the blue, To be hit by a calamity
पहाड़ से टक्कर लेना	To be up against a giant
पहाड़ होना	To be too heavy
पहुँचा पकड़ना	To take undue advantage
पहेली बुझाना	1. To argue to no purpose 2. To pettifog 3. To solve a puzzle
पाँच, तीन (करना)	To put up false pretences
पाँच-सात (करना)	To quarrel
पाँच-सात में पड़ना	To fall into confusion
पाँचों उँगलियाँ घी में होना	1. To be in a prosperous position 2. To be on velvet 3. To have one's bread buttered on both sides
पाँचों उँगलियाँ बराबर नहीं होतीं	All are not alike
पाँचों/पाँचवें सवारों में नाम लिखाना	To consider oneself amongst the chosen few
पाँचवाँ सवार होना	Claiming to belong to a dominant group
पाँव अड़ाना	To hinder, to interfere, to meddle

पाँव उखड़ जाना	Unable to hold one's ground
पाँव उखड़ना	To lose ground, to lose hold
पाँव उखाड़ना	To dislodge
पाँव की धूल होना	Be nothing in comparison with, Not fit to hold a candle to
पाँव गाड़ना	To plant oneself
पाँव घिसना	To be tired
पाँव जमना	To establish oneself firmly
पाँव जमाना	To consolidate one's position
पाँव, जमीन पर (न पड़ना)	To be beside oneself with delight
पाँव डिगना	1. To commit a lapse 2. To falter
पाँव तले की धरती खिसकना	To have cold feet, To be flabbergasted
पाँव पकड़ना	To surrender, To yield
पाँव पड़ना	To entreat
पाँव फूँक-फूँककर रखना	To proceed very cautiously
पाँव भारी होना	To be in a family way (pregnant)
पाँव में कुल्हाड़ी मारना, अपने	1. To cut the branch on which one is sitting 2. To ruin oneself
पाँव में चक्कर होना	To be always on the move
पाँव में मेहँदी लगाना	Not to move anywhere
पाँव समेटना	To withdraw
पाँसा उलटा पड़ना	Situation to be topsy-turvied
पाँसा सीधा पड़ना	To be favoured by luck.

पागलपन सवार होना	To go crazy, To run amuck
पाटों में पिसना, दो	To be pounded between mortar and pestle
पानी आना, मुँह में	Mouth begins to water
पानी उतरना, आँख का	To have lost all shame
पानी का बताशा	1. A water bubble 2. Something empty or not lasting
पानी की तरह बहाना (रुपया)	To play ducks and drakes with (one's money), To squander away
पानी के मोल मिलना	Very cheap ·
पानी-पानी कर देना	To put to shame
पानी-पानी होना	To be overwhelmed with shame
पानी पीकर जात पूछना	Wise after the event
पानी पी-पीकर कोसना	To heap curses upon someone
पानी फिर जाना	To fall to the ground
पानी फेर देना	1. To undo 2. To put a spoke in someone's wheel
पानी, बे (करना)	To disgrace
पानी में आग लगाना	1. To attempt the impossible 2. To cause the impossible to happen 3. To set water on fire
पानी में रहकर मगर से बैर करना	To live in Rome and fight with Pope
पाप का घड़ा	Extremity of sinful deeds

पाप का घड़ा कभी-न-कभी फूटता है	The mills of God grind slowly
पाप की कमाई, कुत्ते-बिल्लियों ने खाई	Ill got, ill spent
पाप की गठरी	Burden of sinful deeds
पापड़ बेलना	1. To undergo hardships 2. To work hard and have little in return
पार उतरना	1. To cope with a difficulty 2. To cross over a river 3. To succeed
पार उतारना	1. To extricate from trouble 2. To see things through
पार पड़ना	To deal successfully with something
पार, बेडा (है)	1. To help getting over a difficulty 2. The worst part is over
पार लगाना/पाना	1. To fathom the depth 2. To get the better
पारा उतरना	1. To be pacified 2. To calm/cool down
पारा गरम होना	To lose temper
पारा चढ़ना	To get infuriated
पालथी मारकर बैठना	To squat cross-legged
पालना, बला	To nurse a nuisance
पाला पड़ना, किसी से	To come in contact with someone, To have to do with someone
पाले पड़ना	1. To fall into the clutches of

	2. To have to do with
पासंग बराबर भी न होना	To be no match for
पासंग भी न होना	Not a patch on, Not in the same street with, Utterly inferior to someone in ability
पास न फटकना	To keep at an arm's length, To maintain a distance, To stay away
पास रखना	1. To appoint 2. To deposit 3. To keep with oneself
पासा / पाँसा पड़ना	To have a good luck
पासा पलट देना	To turn tables on someone
पासा पलटना	1. To go wrong 2. To have a change of fortune
पासा सीधा पड़ना	To have a spell of good luck
पिंड छुड़ाना	To get rid of
पिंड छूटना	To be free, To get riddance
पिंड छोड़ना	1. To leave 2. To let one live in peace
पित्ता मारकर काम करना	To work very hard without distraction
पिद्दी का शोरबा	An insignificant being
पिस जाना	To keep one's nose to the grindstone
पिसना, गेहूँ के साथ घुन	When the buffaloes fight, crops suffer

पीछा करना	To pursue, To tread close upon
पीछा छुड़ाना	To get rid of
पीछा छोड़ना	To desert
पीछा दिखाना	To leave in the lurch
पीछा पकड़ना	To attach oneself to, To hang on the skirts of
पीछा भारी होना	To have a rich background, To have strong support
पीछे पड़ना	1. To chase, to harass, to tease 2. To pursue vigorously
पीछे-पीछे चलना	To follow in the steps of
पीछे लगना	To shadow, To follow the tracks of
पीछे हटना	1. To back out of (one's word) 2. To retreat, to withdraw
पीटना, नाम	To take advantage of one's name
पीठ ठोकना / पर हाथ फेरना	To pat one on the back
पीठ दिखाना	1. To run away from the battle-field 2. To show the white feather 3. To turn tail
पीठ पर होना	1. To be at the back of 2. To be behind one in support
पीठ फेरना	1. To run away from 2. To turn one's back upon
पीठ में छुरा घोंपना/भोंकना	To stab in the back
पीठ लगाना	1. To be thrown flat on the back

	2. To take rest
पीसना, दाँत	To gnash one's teeth
पुट्ठे पर हाथ न रखने देना	To be hard to approach,
	To keep one's distance
पुतला बाँधना	To defame
पुरजा, चलता	1. Clever
	2. Cunning
	3. Resourceful
	4. Shrewd
पुरजा ढीला करना	To serve one right
पुरजे-पुरजे करना	To break into pieces,
	To dismantle,
	To tear to shreds
पुराना घाघ होना	To be an experienced crafty person
पुराना पापी	Old Adam
पुराना रोना धोना	To narrate an old story in detail
पुराना हिसाब चुकाना	1. To pay off old scores
	2. To settle accounts (avenging an injury)
पुरानी लीक पीटना	To follow old traditions
	To tread the off trodden path
पुराने मुरदे उखाड़ना	To dig up old grievances
पुल बाँधना	To extol one to the skies
पुल बाँधना, हवाई (पुलाव पकाना, ख्याली)	To build castles in the air
पूँछ पकड़कर चलना	To follow blindly
पूँछ, बड़ी (का)	1. Resourceful
	2. Well-known

पूछ न होना	To be a nobody, To command no respect
पूछना, बात न	To evince no concern for someone
पूतों फलना	To prosper by leaps and bounds
पूरा उतरना	To come up to one's expectations
पूरा पड़ना	To be sufficient
पूरी नहीं तो आधी भली	Something is better than nothing
पूरे दिन करना	To pass time by hook or by crook To reach the end of one's term
पूरे दिन होना (दिन पूरे)	1. One's time in the world to by over 2. To complete pregnancy term
पेंदी का लोटा, बिना (बे)	1. A person with constantly varying views 2. Rolling stone 3. Unprincipled person
पेच कसना	1. To set right 2. To tighten the loose screw
पेच खाना	To fall into complexities
पेच देना	To give a turn
पेच पड़ना	A complication to arise
पेट का गहरा	One who can stomach a secret
पेट का चक्कर	The daily errand for earning one's bread
पेट काटना	1. To be deprived of one's means of sustenance

	2. To live more thriftily
	3. To tighten one's belt
पेट का पानी न पचाना	1. Unable to digest anything
	2. Unable to keep secrets
पेट का हलका	Unable to keep secrets
पेट की आग	Hunger
पेट की आग बुझाना	To satisfy one's hunger
पेट की बात	Secret, inner secret
पेट गिराना	To cause abortion
पेट पर लात मारना/छुरी चलाना	1. Taking away one's living
	2. To deprive one of one's means of livelihood
पेट में पानी होना	To be fearful
पेट पालना	To earn one's living somehow, To keep body and soul together
पेट में चूहे कूदना	To be awfully hungry, To suffer the pangs of hunger
पेट में दाढ़ी होना	1. To be very astute
	2. To have an old head over young shoulders
पेट में बल पड़ना	To be rolled about with laughter, To roll in the aisles
पेट रहना	To be pregnant
पेट से पाँव निकालना	To go beyond decent bounds, To go beyond limits
पेटा भरना	To have one's fill
पेटी उतरना	To be dismissed
पैंतरा बदलना	To shift one's ground,

	To change one's stance, To change one's strategy, Volte-face
पैर उखड़ना	Not being able to hold one's ground, To be in a fix
पैर की जूती/धूल	Of no significance, worthless
पैर पकड़ना	To beseech
पैर बढ़ाना	To move forward
पैर भारी होना	To be pregnant
पैरों पर खड़े होना	To depend entirely on oneself, To stand on one's own legs
पैरों में छाले पड़ना	Blistering caused by continuous hard work or long journeys covered on foot
पैसा उड़ाना	To squander away
पैसा खा जाना	1. To embezzle 2. To take bribe
पैसा डुबोना	To lose one's money irretrievably
पैसा लगाना	To invest money
पैसे के सब यार	1. A full purse never lacks friends 2. When good cheers are lacking, friends will be packing
पैसे-पैसे को तरसना	To be hard up, To be too tight
पोंगा पंडित	Brainless fellow
पों बोलना	To admit defeat

पोतड़ों का रईस	Born with a silver spoon in one's mouth
पोल खुलना	1. Exposure of inner secret 2. The cat is out of the bag
पोल खोल देना/खोलना	To expose, to reveal a secret
पोल, ढोल की	High sounding without, hollow within
पौ बारह होना	1. To attain prosperity/success 2. To become rich suddenly
प्यासा, खून का	Blood thirsty, Sworn enemy
प्यासे को ही कुएँ के पास जाना पड़ता है	If the mountain will not come to Mohammad, Mohammad will go to the mountain
प्रकाश करना	To illuminate
प्रकाश में लाना	To bring to light
प्रणाम, दूर से (करना)	To avoid, To keep at an arm's length, To maintain a safe distance
प्रलय मचाना	To cause havoc, To raise an uproar
प्रेम गली अति साँकरी	The path of love is very narrow and strewn with thorns
प्रेम ही प्रेम का पुरस्कार	Love is its own reward

फ

फंदे में आना/पड़ना/फँसना	To fall into the clutches of
फँसना, किसी से	1. To be entangled with someone 2. To develop illicit relations with someone
फँसना, किसी से (चंगुल)	To be caught in someone's trap
फँसना, बुरा	1. To be caught in a difficulty 2. To be entrapped
फक, रंग (पड़ जाना)	1. To be non-plussed 2. To turn pale
फकीर करना	To reduce to beggary
फकीर होना, लकीर का	Conservative
फटकना, पास नहीं	To keep away
फट पड़ना	1. To burst into anger/rebuke/ tears 2. To grow fat suddenly
फटना, छाती	To fall victim to green-eyed god
फटना, मन	To be disillusioned, To be estranged
फटना, सिर	To have severe headache
फड़क उठना	To be thrilled with joy

फतूर उठाना/खड़ा करना	To kick up a row
फतूर चढ़ना	To be obsessed by an irrational desire
फतूर, दिमाग में	1. To go crazy about something 2. Unsoundness of mind
फन, हर (मौला) (सर्वगुण संपन्न)	Master of all trades
फफोले फोड़ना, दिल के	1. To give vent to one's suppressed feelings 2. To remember one's sores aloud
फरक आना	Misunderstanding to arise (between)
फर्राटे भरना/मारना	1. To move swiftly 2. To take rapid strides
फर्राटे से बोलना	To speak fluently
फल चखना	To face the consequences (of)
फल पाना	1. To be rewarded 2. To face the result of 3. To suffer for one's sins
फल होना	To be the outcome of
फसाद खड़ा करना	To kick up a row
फाकों का मारा	A starving person
फाकों मरना	To die of starvation
फाकों से रहना	1. To face acute shortage of food 2. To live in starvation
फाख्ता होना, होश	To lose one's wits
फिकर (फिक्र) में रहना	To be constantly worrying
फिरकी की तरह फिरना	To go round non-stop

फिरना, झाड़ू	To be despoiled completely, To lose all that one had
फिरना, दिन	Days to take a turn for the better, Fortune to smile
फिरना, बात से	To back out of one's word
फिरना, सिर	To lose one's cool
फिस्स, टाँय टाँय	Ending in a flop
फिस्स हो जाना	To come to naught
फीका	Dull, uninteresting
फीका पड़ना	To lose lustre
फीका लगना	To appear tasteless
फुर्र हो जाना	To disappear abruptly
फुलझड़ी छोड़ना	1. To make the fur fly 2. To pass a provocative remark 3. To stir up trouble
फुलाना, गाल/मुँह	To be sulky/angry
फूँक तमाशा देखना, घर	To fiddle while Rome burns
फूँक निकल जाना	1. To be frightened 2. To expire
फूँक निकालना	1. To deflate 2. To frighten
फूँक-फूँककर कदम/पैर रखना	1. To proceed with caution 2. To progress slowly
फूँक, मारते ही	In a jiffy
फूँकना, जान	To put life into
फूँकना, माल	To spend money
फूँक-सा	Frail
फूटना, किस्मत	To have a stroke of bad luck

फूटी आँख न देखना/सुहाना	There is no love lost between them
फूटी कौड़ी पास न होना	1. Not to have a bean, 2. To be a pauper
फूटे मुँह बात न करना	1. Not to speak on any account 2. Not to talk even by way of courtesy
फूलकर कुप्पा हो जाना	To be elated, to be overjoyed
फूल के साथ काँटे होना	No rose without thorns
फूल झड़ना	To speak sweetly/eloquently
फूल सूँघकर जीना	To be too abstemious
फूला न समाना	To be too happy to contain oneself
फूला-फूला फिरना	To give oneself airs
फूला होना	To be angry with
फूले अंग न समाना	To be overjoyed, to be too happy
फूले न समाना	1. On top of the world 2. Unable to contain oneself with joy
फूस का तापना	A vain attempt
फूस में चिनगारी डालना	To foment trouble, To stir the embers
फेंटा कसना	To get ready for any eventuality, To gird up one's loins
फेर, निन्यानवे का	Excessive greed of wealth, To run in pursuit of money
फेर में डालना	1. To deceive 2. To involve in a maze 3. To mislead

फेर में पड़ना/होना	To get involved in a complication
फेर लेना, आँखें	To turn one's eyes away
फेर, समझ का	Matter of opinion
फेर, समय का	Irony of fate, The times to take a turn
फेरना, कलम	To write off
फेरना, जबान	To go back on one's word
फेरना, माला	To till beads
फेरना, हाथ	To caress, To fondle, To soothe
फेरे डालना/पड़ना	To be tied in a nuptial knot
फेरे लगाना	To take frequent rounds (business)
फैलाना, मुँह	To demand exorbitantly
फैलाना, हाथ	1. To ask something humbly 2. To beg for something
फोड़ना, गवाह	To allure a witness to one's side
फोड़ना, भंडा	1. To disclose, to divulge 2. To reveal a secret

ब

बंदर की दोस्ती	Fickle friendship
बंदर घुड़की	Hollow/Empty threats
बकरे की माँ कब तक खैर मनाएगी ?	What is allotted cannot be blotted
बखिया उधेड़ना	To reveal a secret
बगल गरम करना	To go to bed with
बगल में ईमान दबाना	To adopt dishonest means
बगल में गरदन झुकाना	To be ashamed
बगल में छुरी मुँह में राम	Wolf in lamb's skin, Wolf in sheep's clothing
बगल में दबाना	To conceal in one's armpit
बगला / बगुला भगत	1. A canting hyprocrite 2. A pious fraud
बगली देना	To make hole in a house wall to enter
बगलें झाँकना	1. To be cornered 2. To be non-plussed/perplexed 3. To look blank
बगलें बजाना	To crow over, To dance with joy,

	To manifest delight
बगावत का झंडा उठाना	To raise the banner of revolt
बगुला भगत बनना	To sail under false colours
बघारना, शेखी	To behave arrogantly, To brag
बचना, बाल-बाल	To have a narrow escape
बछिया के दाँत नहीं देखे जाते, दान की	1. Beggars should not be choosers 2. To find fault with a gift 3. To look a gift horse in the mouth
बजाकर देखना, ठोक	To test thoroughly as to the work and worth
बट्टा लगाना, नाम को	To cast a slur on, To tarnish one's reputation
बट्टे-खाते डालना	To write off as bad debt
बड़ी-बड़ी बातों से पेट नहीं भरता	Fine words butter no parsnips, Words do not fill the belly
बड़े घर की हवा खिलाना	To be sent to jail, To have a taste of prison house
बड़े बोल बोलना	To boast, To indulge in bravado
बड़े लोग छोटा काम नहीं करते	An eagle does not hawk at flies
बड़ाई जताना	To boast of superiority
बड़ों-बड़ों से लोहा लेना	To cross swords with big guns
बड़ों की बातें भी बड़ी	High winds blow up high hills
बढ़-चढ़कर बोलना	1. To brag, To speak boastfully 2. To raise one's bid

बढ़ा-चढ़ाकर कहना	1. To draw the long bow 2. To exaggerate 3. To throw the hatchet
बढ़ा-चढ़ाकर लड़ा देना	To incite to fight
बतंगड़, बात का	Much ado about nothing, Storm in a tea cup
बताशा-सा घुलना	To fade away
बत्तीसी झाड़ना	To knock out the teeth
बत्तीसी दिखाना	To guffaw, To show full set of one's teeth
बद अच्छा, बदनाम बुरा	A bad name is worse than wickedness
बदन में आग लगना	To be enraged
बदन हरा होना	To be refreshed
बदमाशी करना	To play the Jack
बदलना, बात	To change one's stand
बदला चुकाना (हिसाब)	To retaliate, To square accounts with
बधिया बैठना	1. Crashing of a business 2. Crippling loss to be sustained 3. To be ruined 4. To suffer an irreparable loss
बन आना	To have the best of both worlds
बना-ठना	Spick and span
बना रहना	1. To carry on 2. To remain unchanged
बरस पड़ना	1. To abuse one unexpectedly 2. To attack one suddenly and violently

	3. To lash out at
बल पर कूदना, किसी के	To thunder on the strength of others
बला टालना	To ward off an evil
बला, मेरी (से)	Damn it, I care a fig! I'm damned if I know!
बला मोल लेना	To invite trouble
बला है, तू क्या	You are worth nothing
बलि का बकरा	1. Cannon fodder 2. Scape goat 3. To be left to suffer the consequences of other's deeds 4. Whipping boy
बल्लियों उछलना	Joy knowing no bounds, To be on the high ropes
बल्लियों उछालना	To be beside oneself with delight
बवंडर उठाना	1. To create confusion 2. To raise a storm
बवंडर, बात का (खड़ा करना)	To create a storm in a tea cup, To make a mountain of a mole hill
बवंडर मचना / मचाना	To create havoc
बस चलना	To have one's say
बसाना, घर (अपना)	Start leading a married life
बस्ता बाँधना	1. To pack one's belongings, 2. To send somebody packing 3. To wind up day's work

बहती गंगा में हाथ धोना	1. Make hay while the sun shines 2. Strike when the iron is hot
बहाना, पानी की तरह पैसा	To play ducks and drakes with one's money
बहार देना	To lend splendour
बहार पर आना	To bloom
बहार पर होना	To be in full bloom/glory
बहार लूटना	To enjoy the delights
बहुत से जोगी मठ उजाड़ें	Too many cooks spoil the broth
बाँका, बाल (न होने देना)	To emerge unscathed
बाँछें खिलना	To feel extremely happy
बाँट, बंदर	1. A distribution weighted in favour of oneself 2. An unfair distribution in which parties lose and arbiter gains
बाँटे पड़ना	To fall to one's share
बाँधना, गाँठ	To note as a warning
बाँधना, तारीफ के पुल	To praise to the skies
बाँबी में हाथ देना	To invite trouble
बाँस, उलटे (बरेली को)	To carry coal to New castle
बाँस पर चढ़ना	To be held in bad light
बाँस पर चढ़ाना	1. To hold up to disgrace 2. To praise someone highly with intent to wrest some favour from him
बाँसों उछलना/कूदना	1. His joy knows no bounds

	2. To go into an ecstasy of delight
बाएँ हाथ का खेल	Child's play
बाएँ होना	1. To be adversely disposed
	2. To be against, to be opposed
	3. To be hostile
बागडोर हाथ में होना	1. To have control
	2. To hold the reins of
बागडोर हाथ से छूटना	1. To lose control
	2. To lose hold over the reins of
बागी हो जाना	To fly in the face of
बाछें खिलना	To be extremely happy, to be manifestly delighted
बाज आना	To desist from, to give up
बाजार उतरना	1. Market to be in a state of depression
	2. Prices to fall
बाजार गरम होना	1. Prices to shoot up
	2. Marketing activities to be in full swing
बाजार गिरना	1. Market to be slack
	2. Prices to drop
बाजारी खबर	Mere rumour
बाजी खाना	To lose
बाजी मारना/जीतना	1. To bear the palm
	2. To take a cake
	3. To score a victory
	4. To sweep the board, to win

बाजी लें जाना	1. To emerge victorious 2. To excel 3. To steal a march on 4. To surpass
बाजी हारना	1. To be beaten hollow 2. To be defeated 3. To lose a bet
बाट मारना	1. To rob 2. To waylay
बाट रोकना	To block one's way
बाढ़ पर चढ़ना	To instigate, To provoke
बात अखरना	To feel bad about something
बात आई-गई होना	1. The matter is closed 2. The matter is hushed up
बात उठा न रखना	To spare no effort on one's part
बात उठाना	To raise a matter
बात उड़ना	A rumour to go round
बात उलटना	To contradict
बात ऊँची रखना	To keep one's word
बात का कच्चा	Untrue to one's word
बात का धनी/पक्का	A man of his word
बात का बतंगड़ बनाना	1. To exaggerate 2. To raise a storm in a tea-cup
बात काटना	To cut one short, to interrupt
बात-की-बात में	In an instant, forthwith
बात की तह तक पहुँचना	To get to the bottom of the matter

बात को ताड़ लेना	1. To perceive the matter in real terms 2. To understand the matter in proper perspective
बात को छिपाना	To conceal the matter, To obscure the truth
बात कान में डालना	To bring into one's notice
बात चलाना	To broach the subject
बात छीनना	To take the very word out of one's mouth
बात छेड़ना	To initiate
बात जमना	Matter to take some shape
बात न पूछना	To ignore, not to take any notice
बात बढ़ाना	To aggravate the matter
बात-बात में	In almost every thing
बात बिगाड़ना	To worsen the matter
बात रखना	To honour one's word
बात लाख की, करनी खाक की	A long tongue has a short hand
बात से मुकरना	To go back on one's words, To eat one's words
बातें गढ़ना	To fabricate
बातें मिलाना	To tell tales
बातें लगाना	To indulge in backbiting
बातें सुनना	To hear (abuse) uncomplainingly
बातों से पेट नहीं भरता	1. Belly has no ears 2. Fine words butter no parsnips 3. Mere words will not fill a bushel
बातों में बात निकालना	To read between the lines

बातें पाना	To understand
बातें बनाना	To concoct tales, to make lame excuses
बातें मानना	To accept someone's suggestions
बातों-बातों में	1. By the way 2. In the course of conversation
बातों में आना	To be taken in
बातों में उड़ाना	1. To outwit 2. To talk somebody out
बातों में फँसाना	To entrap one by talking
बातों में बहलाना	To win one over by one's oily tongue
बादलों में थिगली लगाना	To accomplish the impossible
बादलों से बातें करना	To be almost touching the sky
बान डालना	1. To accustom 2. To cultivate a habit
बानक बनना	1. Things to take the desired shape 2. To have things move along expected lines
बाना बदलना	To disguise oneself
बाप का माल समझना	To regard something as one's own father's property
बाप-दादा का नाम डुबोना	To bring bad name to one's family
बाप बनाना, अंधे को	To flatter every Tom, Dick and Harry to achieve one's ends
बार देना	To give access to
बारह बाँट करना	1. To scatter

	2. To sow the seeds of strife
बारह बाँट होना	To be rendered homeless
बारीकियाँ छाँटना	1. To go into minute details 2. To make captious criticism
बाल की खाल निकालना	1. To indulge in hair-splitting 2. To make subtle distinctions
बाल नोचना	To tear one's hair
बाल पकना, धूप में	To age without experience
बाल बराबर होना	Hair breadth, Negligible, slightest
बाल बाँका न होना	To come out unscathed, To remain unhurt
बाल बाल कर्ज में होना	To be over head and ears in debt
बाल-बाल बचना	To have a narrow escape
बाल-भर भी फर्क न होना	Not to have the least difference
बालू की दीवार	1. A house of cards 2. An infirm structure 3. Anything not to be relied on
बालू से तेल निकालना	1. To engage in hopeless enterprise 2. To extract money from a miser 3. To milk the bull 4. To wring blood from a stone 5. To wring water from a flint
बावन तोले पाव रत्ती	1. Absolutely exact 2. Precise and proper 3. Precisely correct

बासी कढ़ी में उबाल आना	Young ways in old age
बासी बचे न कुत्ता खाए	To live from hand to mouth
बाहर की हवा लगना	To adopt wrong ways
बाहरं भेजना	To send abroad
बाहर होना	1. To be excluded 2. To dissent from
बाहर होना, आपे से	To be beside oneself with rage
बिकना, किसी के हाथ	1. To surrender oneself completely to someone 2. To be under somebody's complete control
बिगड़ खड़ा होना	To become angry suddenly
बिगुल बजाना	To sound a bugle (to signal an expedition etc. to commence)
बिच्छू का मंत्र न जाने, साँप के बिल उँगली डाले	Bare-footed men should not tread on thorns
बिछाना, आँखें/पलकें	To accord a cordial welcome
बिदा (विदा) करना	1. To bid farewell 2. To dismiss 3. To say good bye
बिना चावल के खीर पकाना	To do something without the necessary material, To make bricks without straw
बिना बात की बात	1. For nothing 2. Talk of no consequence
बिना लाग-लपेट के	Without any fear or favour
बिना विचारे जो करे, सो पाछे पछताय	Look before you leap
बिना सेवा मेवा नहीं मिलता	No gain without pain

बिरते, किस (पर)	On what basis? With whose support?
बिरते पर उछलना	To bask in the reflected glory
बिल्ली के गले में घंटी बाँधना/ रस्सी बाँधना	To bell the cat
बिल्ली के भागों छींका टूटना	1. Fortune to smile on the needy 2. How can the cat help if the maid be a fool ?
बिल्ली के सिरहाने दूध नहीं जमता	1. A watched pot never boils 2. Watching and anxiety won't hasten matters
बिल्ली गई चूहों की बन आई	Mice play when the cat is away
बिल्ली, मेरी (और मुझको ही म्याऊँ?)	Does he/she presume to question me?
बिल्ली से छीछड़ों की रखवाली	To set a fox to keep the geese
बिसात, उसकी क्या (कि?)	How can he have the means...?
बिसात से बाहर काम करना	To bite off more than one can chew
बिस्तर गोल करना	1. To clear out bag and baggage 2. To pack up
बिस्तर बाँधना	To pack off
बीच-बचाव/बिचाव करना	To mediate
बीच में आना	To intervene
बीच में कूद पड़ना	To interfere
बीच में बोलना	To interrupt
बीज बोना	To give rise to, To sow seeds of
बीड़ा उठाना/लेना	To accept a challenge solemnly

बाजी मार लेना	To bear the palm
बीन बजाना, भैंस के आगे	To cast pearls before a swine
बुझाना, दिल की लगी	To feed the flame of love
बुढ़ापे का सहारा	Only support of old age
बुत रहना	To keep silent
बुत हो जाना	To keep mum
बुरा बनाना	To lower one in the estimation of
बुरा-भला कहना	To scold severely
बुरा मानना	To take amiss
बुरा हाल करना	1. To maltreat 2. To reduce to a sad state 3. To ruin
बुरी आदतें पड़ना आसान है, जाना मुश्किल	The road to hell is easy
बुरी तरह खबर लेना	To give one a good thrashing
बुरी तरह पेश आना	To maltreat
बुरी तरह लताड़ना	To give one hell
बुरे दिन आना	To fall on evil times
बूँद-बूँद से घड़ा/तालाब भरता है	Many a drop makes an ocean, Many a little makes a mickle, Slow and steady wins the race
बूढ़ी घोड़ी, लाल लगाम	1. Elderly woman got up to look young 2. Mutton dressed like a lamb 3. Old age, young ways
बूढ़े तोते भी पढ़ते हैं ?	Old dogs will not learn new tricks
बूते से बाहर होना	To be beyond one's power

बेकार से बेगार भली	Forced labour is better than idleness, Something is better than nothing
बेड़ा डूबना	1. An enterprise/concern to fail 2. To be ruined/undone
बेड़ा पार होना	1. To achieve the goal 2. To see one through a difficulty
बेनकाब हो जाना	To throw off the mask, To unmask
बेपर की उड़ाना	1. To spread baseless rumours 2. To talk tall
बेपेंदी का लोटा	1. An unprincipled person 2. Unsteady 3. Wavering mind 4. Weather cock
बेबाक कर देना	To square accounts with
बेभाव की पड़ना	To be beaten severely
बेमौत मारा जाना	To be completely undone
बेल मढ़े चढ़ना	1. To flourish by leaps and bounds 2. To reach consummation
बे सिर-पैर का	1. One having no basis 2. Irrelevent (remarks)
बे सिर-पैर की हाँकना	1. To beat about the bush 2. To talk nonsense
बैठते, उठते	All the time

बैठना, ठीक	To carry conviction
बैठाना, लागत	To calculate the cost
बैठाना, हाथ	To acquire the needed skill, To practise
बैठाना, हिसाब	To settle the accounts
बैठे-ठाले से बेगार भली	Unremunerated work is better than no work, Something is better than nothing
बैरंग लौटना	To fail in one's mission and return back
बैर बोना	To sow seeds of enmity
बैर मोल लेना	To invite animosity
बैल की तरह पिलना/पिसना	To work like a horse
बैल दुहना	To milk the bull
बैल मुझे मार, आ	To ask for trouble
बोझ उतरना	A burden to be off one's chest
बोझ उतार देना	To fulfil an obligation
बोझ उतारना	To relieve oneself of a burden
बोटी-बोटी फड़कना	To be restive, To be thrilled
बोतल चढ़ाना	To drink
बोरिया-बिस्तर बाँधना	1. To pack bag and baggage 2. To prepare oneself to leave
बोल चबाना	To eat one's word
बोल जाना	To feel exhausted
बोल बोलना, बड़े	To indulge in tall talks
बोल-बाला	1. Sway, high repute, pre-eminence

	2. To be the order of the day
बोल मारना	To make sarcastic remarks, To taunt
बोलती बंद कर देना	To render one tight-lipped
बोलती बंद हो जाना	To become speechless
बोली बोलना	1. To bid 2. To make fun of 3. To pass taunting remarks
बौराना, मत (बुद्धि)	1. Mind to have gone on wool gathering 2. To become crazy 3. To go off one's head
ब्याही तबही जानिये जब डोली जावे	Many a slip between the cup and the lip
ब्योंत बैठाना	To adjust things, To manoeuvre plan

भंडा फूटना	A secret to be exposed
भंडा-फोड़	Disclosure of secret
भंड़ा-फोड़ करना	1. To blow the gaff 2. To disclose a secret 3. To uncover a plot
भँवर-जाल में फँसना	1. To be entangled in a mess 2. To get into a state of turmoil
भगत, बगुला	A canting hypocrite
भगवान् को प्यारा होना	To pass away
भगीरथ प्रयत्न करना	To make herculean efforts
भड़भड़ मचाना	To create an uproar
भड़ास निकालना	1. To blow off steam 2. To give vent to one's suppressed feelings/stored up spite 3. To unburden one's mind
भनक पड़ना / लगना	1. To get a clue to 2. To get a faint sound 3. To get an inkling of
भभकी देना, बंदर	To hold out a hollow threat

भर आना, जी	Soul to be moved by compassion
भर जाना, पाँव	To get tired
भर पाना	To be paid in full
भरना, आँखें	To be moved to tears
भरना, कान	To backbite To poison one's ears
भरना, किसी को	To poison the mind of someone
भरना, गोद	To be blessed with a child
भरना, जी / मन	To be satisfied in ample measure
भरना, पापों का घड़ा	The vessel of sins to be overbrimming
भरम बनाये रखना	To keep up appearances
भरा बैठना	To be in full rage
भरी थाली पर लात मारना	To discard an affluent position
भला बुरा कहना	To scold
भांडा फूटना	To be exposed, A secret to be revealed
भाग्य खुलना/जगना	Fortune to take a favourable turn
भाग्य-फूटना	To be visited by ill luck
भाड़ झोंकना	To do a worthless task, to waste one's time in useless pursuits
भाड़ नहीं फूटता, एक चने से	One swallow does not make a summer
भाड़ में जाए	Be damned! Go to hell! Let him go to hell
भाड़ में झोंकना	To bring to ruin
भाड़े का टट्टू	Mercenary

भानुमती का कुनबा	An unusual assortment of different kinds of elements, Startlingly odd collection
भानुमती का पिटारा	A box containing amazing variety of odd things, A wonder casket
भाना, फूटी आँखों नहीं	To be an eye-sore
भार उठाना	To take up a responsibility
भार उतारना	1. To throw a burden off one's head 2. To unburden
भार डालना	To entrust responsibility
भार होना	To be burdensome
भारी, पैर (होना)	To be in the family way
भारी रहना	1. To be dominating 2. To be more than a match 3. To be stronger
भारी लगना	To appear to be a burden
भिगो-भिगोकर मारना/लगाना	1. To defeat one without compunction 2. To give a thorough beating 3. To pay mocking respects 4. To scold a person
भिड़ के छत्ते में हाथ डालना	To invite troubles, To stir up a hornet's nest
भीगी बिल्ली बनना	1. To appear meek and humble 2. To be over-submissive
भीत, बालू की	A house of cards, An ill-conceived scheme

भुजा उठाना	To take a vow
भुट्टा-सा उड़ना	To be cut clean off, To be removed from the scene with striking suddenness
भुस में आग लगाय जमालो दूर खड़ी	To be casual after causing a crisis, To join the spectators after causing a fire-break
भूख में किवाड़ पापड़	Hunger is the best sauce
भूख में गूलर पकवान	It does not pay to be dainty when hungry
भूख में चने भी मखाने	Hungry dogs will eat dirty pudding
भूत बनना	To be a work-horse
भूत सवार होना	1. To be obsessed by 2. To get crazy after 3. To have a bee in one's bonnet
भूत होना	To work like a ghost
भूल सुधारना	To make amends
भूले को अब याद मत करो	Let sleeping dogs lie
भूसा भरा होना, दिमाग में	Brainless fellow, One whose brain is stuffed with straws
भृकुटी टेढ़ी होना	To be visibly annoyed
भेंट करना	To give an interview
भेंट चढ़ जाना	To be sacrificed
भेजा खाना (बकबक कर सिर खाना)	1. To bore by continual dull talk 2. To bother too much with trivial queries etc.

	3. To pester
भेड़ चाल	Mass imitation, Mob mentality
भैंस बराबर	An extra-fat woman
भौंहें चढ़ाना/टेढ़ी करना/तानना	To frown, to scowl
भौचक्का रह जाना/हक्का बक्का	To be taken aback (surprised)
भ्रम खुलना	To be disillusioned
भ्रम में डालना	To confuse, To mislead

मंजिल पहुँचना	To reach one's destination
मंझधार में छोड़ना	To leave in the lurch
मंद पड़ना	To be pacified
मक्खन लगाना	To butter up, To flatter, To lay it on thick
मक्खियाँ उड़ाना	To kill time
मक्खियाँ मारना	1. To engage in useless activities 2. To idle away time 3. To twiddle one's thumbs
मक्खी की तरह निकाल बाहर करना	1. To reject somebody outright 2. To remove someone unwanted 3. To throw out the persona-non-grata
मक्खी के स्थान पर मक्खी	To be foolishly letter-bound, To be literal
मक्खी, जीती (निगलना)	To tolerate a wrong thing being said right

मक्खी न बैठने देना, नाक पर	1. To react sharply 2. To wish to be not less than perfect
मक्खी निगलना	To suffer a wrong with eyes open
मखौल समझना	To take something to be too easy
मगज खाना/चाटना	To pester with constant babble
मगज खाली करना	To talk a person's head off
मगज मारना	To make an intensive mental effort, To tax one's brain
मगर, अगर (करना)	To indulge in ifs and buts
मछली की तरह तड़पना	To feel like fish out of water
मजा उड़ाना	To enjoy oneself to the full
मजा किरकिरा होना	To mar all the pleasure of
मजा चखाना	1. To teach one a good lesson 2. To settle score
मजा लूटना	1. To enjoy oneself 2. To make fun
मजाक उड़ाना	To laught at, To make fun of
मजाक में उड़ा देना	To laugh off
मजाक समझना	To treat as fun
मजे करना	To have a whale of a time
मजे की बात	Something pleasant
मजे में रहना	To lead a contented life
मजे से रहना	To live in clover
मटियामेट करना	To destroy, To ruin

मढ़ना, किसी के सिर/मत्थे	1. To ascribe to 2. To attribute to 3. To impose on someone
मतलब की बात करना	To get down to brass tacks
मतलब गाँठना	1. To have an axe to grind 2. To serve one's own end
मतलब निकालना	To achieve one's objective
मतलब रखना	To have a motive
मत्था टेकना	To bow in reverence
मत्था पच्ची करना	To tax one's brain
मधुर बानी दगाबाज की निशानी	Too much courtesy, too much craft
मन अटकना/उलझना/आना	To fall for, To fall in love (with)
मन उखड़ना/उकताना	To be estranged, To be fed up
मन उचटना	To be filled with disgust
मन उठना	To be displeased, To be no longer interested
मन उड़ना	To be unsteady
मन कचोटना	Conscience to prick, To suffer from a lingering agony
मन कच्चा करना	To feel discouraged, To lose heart
मन कड़ा करना	1. To adopt a stiff attitude 2. To be determined
मन का काला	Black-hearted
मन का बोझ हलका करना	To take a load off one's mind

मन का मारा	Dejected, Low-spirited
मन का मैला	Deceitful, Evil-hearted
मन की गाँठ खोल देना	To bare one's heart, To speak open-heartedly
मन की बात	A secret that one cherishes in one's mind
मन की मन में रहना	A wish that did not materialise
मन के लड्डू खाना/फोड़ना	1. To build castles in the air 2. To live in fool's paradise
मन खट्टा हो जाना	1. To be estranged, to be offended 2. To feel utterly displeased
मन खराब होना	To be out of sorts
मनगढंत कहानी	Cock and bull story
मन चलना	To be captivated, to long, to crave
मन छोटा करना	To feel disheartened
मन टटोलना	To probe one's mind, To throw a feeler
मन डिगना	To be swept off
मन डोलना	1. To be attracted 2. To lose self-restraint
मन तोड़ना	To depress
मन देना	To be attentive to
मन नाचने लगना	To go into ecstasies
मन पक्का करना	To make a firm determination

मन पर लाना	To resolve
मन फट जाना/ फटना	1. To be disillusioned
	2. To have a rift
मन फिरना	To be estranged,
	To lose interest
मन बढ़ना	To gain confidence
मन बहलाना	To amuse oneself
मन बिदक जाना	To be averted,
	To turn away from
मन बुरा करना	To be dejected,
	To be displeased
मन भरना	To be fed up, to be satisfied
मन भा जाना	To take fancy to
मन भाना	To be pleasing to the mind
मन भारी करना/होना	To feel heavy-hearted
मन मसोस कर रह जाना	To be agonisingly helpless,
	To suffer anguish of disappointment
मन मानना	To agree,
	To reconcile oneself to
मन मारना (अपना)	1. To suffer patiently
	2. To suppress one's feelings
मन मिलना	To be congenial and friendly
मन मिलाना	To be in agreement with,
	To be one with
मन-मुटाव	1. Bad blood
	2. Ill-feeling
मन में आना	To occur to one's mind
मन में गाँठ पड़ना	1. To develop complex

	2. No longer on old cordil relations
मन में चोर होना	To have a lurking suspicion
मन में ठानना	To resolve
मन में मैल रखना	To bear malice
मन रमना	To be absorbed
मन लगना	To feel at home
मन ललचाना	To crave for, To long for
मन से उतरना	To be liked no more
मन हरा होना	To cheer up, to feel happy
मन हलका होना	1. To feel light 2. To feel a sense of relief
मन-ही-मन	1. In one's heart of hearts 2. Secretly 3. Within one's heart/mind
मन-ही-मन हँसना	To laugh in one's sleeve
मन होना	To have one's heart in
मनसूबा बाँधना	To contrive a plan, To indulge in day-dreaming
मनाना, खैर	1. To pray for the safety of someone 2. To thank one's stars
मनोरथ सिद्ध होना	To fulfil one's desire
मर खप जाना	1. To be dead and gone 2. To toil very hard
मर पचना	To sacrifice one's life
मर मिटना	To be ruined
मरता क्या न करता	1. Driven to the wall, one has no option but to strike back

	2. Necessity knows no law
	3. To have one's back to the wall
मरते-गिरते रहना	1. To live precariously
	2. To manage to survive
मरना, देश पर	To lay down one's life for the sake of one's country
मरने पर छोटे-बड़े एक समान	Death is the great leveller
मरे को मारना	1. To flog a dead horse
	2. To hit a man when he is down
मरे बिना स्वर्ग देखने को नहीं मिलता	He who would eat the nut must first crack the shell
मलते रह जाना, हाथ	To wring one's hands in despair
मशाल लेकर ढूँढ़ना	To search with all the attention at one's command
मस्का मारना/लगाना	To butter up, to flatter
मस्त मौला	A carefree person, Easy-going person
मस्त रहना	To lead a carefree life
मस्तक ऊँचा होना	To feel proud of, To have one's head held high
मस्तक झुकाना	To bow one's head in reverence
मस्तक नीचा होना	To lower one's head out of shame
मस्ती छाना	To be in a hilarious mood
मस्ती झाड़ देना	To cut one to size
मस्ती झाड़ना	To be in high spirits
मस्ती लेना	To take life easy

महफिल उखाड़ना	1. To cause the assembly to disperse
	2. To disrupt the gathering
	3. To mar the show
महफिल गरम होना	Gathering to gain momentum
महफिल जमना	Gathering to be in full swing
महफिल जमाना	To organise a gathering
माँग[१] उजड़ना/सूनी होना	To become widow
माँग[२]-ताँग करना	To ask for, to beg
माँग-पर-माँग होना	To be in great demand
माँजना, हाथ	To improve one's skill by practice
माई-बाप मानना	To regard someone as the only source of help
माथा कूटना	To bewail
माथा खपाना	To tax one's brain
माथा खाना	1. To harass
	2. To subject one to a lot of mental strain
माथा गरम होना	To lose one's temper
माथा टेकना	1. To kowtow
	2. To yield
माथा ठनकना	1. To get an inkling of something fishy
	2. To have a premonition
	3. To smell a rat
माथा रगड़ना	To knowtow
	To prostrate oneself
माथा पकड़कर बैठ जाना	To feel utterly helpless

माथे पर बल न पड़ने देना	Not to show any sign of displeasure, To remain unruffled
माथे पर सेहरा बँधना	1. To be tied in a nuptial knot 2. To get credit for
माथे मढ़ना	1. To attribute to 2. To impose on someone 3. To heap all blame at someone's door
माथे, सिर (बात)	As commanded, As you wish!
मान मनाना	To placate
मान रखना	To honour, To obey
मान रहना	One's honour to be maintained
मामला खटाई में पड़ना	Matter to be put in cold storage, Matter to hang fire
मामला ठंडा / ढीला पड़ना	Matter to lose its urgency, Matter to slacken
मामला तूल पकड़ना	Matter to get aggravated
मामला पक्का करना	To conclude a deal
मामला बनना	To strike a deal
माया आनी-जानी है	Riches have wings
माया को माया मिले कर-कर लंबे हाथ	Money begets money
माया में फँसना	To be attached to things mundane
मारधाड़ मचाना	To unleash violence

मार रखना	To withhold
मार लेना	To usurp
मारना, काठ	To be petrified, To be stunned
मारना, झक	1. To act pointlessly 2. To find no way out 3. To idle away one's time
मारना, डींग	To boast, To talk tall
मारना, तीर	To achieve
मारना, नजर	To cast a glance
मारना, बोली	To pass a remark
मारना, भाँजी	To speak slanderously about someone to sabotage his plan
मारना, मक्खियाँ	To idle away one's time
मारना, मजे	To enjoy oneself, To have a jolly good time
मारना, मन	To practise self-denial To suppress one's desires
मारना, सिर	To rack one's brain
मारना, हाथ-पैर (पाँव)	1. To make efforts 2. To struggle
मार-मार कर आदमी बनाना	To chisel one into a shape
मारा-मार करना	To hasten, To work against time
मारा-मारा फिरना	1. To knock about from pillar to post 2. To live wretchedly

	3. To wander aimlessly
मार्ग में रोड़े अटकाना	To put impediments in the way
मार्ग से भटकाना	To lead astray
माल उड़ाना	1. To consume dainties 2. To misappropriate
माल कटना	Goods to be sold in large quantities
माल मारना	To embezzle
मिजाज खराब होना	To be out of one's element
मिजाज न मिलना	To be ever cross
मिजाज पूछना	To enquire about one's health
मिजाज बिगड़ना	To grow irritated, To lose temper
मिजाज में आना	To come back to one's element
मिजाज शरीफ?	How are you?
मिट्टी उठना	To pass away
मिट्टी का महल बनाना	Make bricks without straw, Set to work without adequate means
मिट्टी का माधो (माधव)	Blithering idiot
मिट्टी का लौंदा	Good for nothing, Worthless fellow
मिट्टी के शेर के मोल	At throw-away price
मिट्टी ठिकाने लगाना	To perform the funeral rites
मिट्टी डालना	To conceal a crime
मिट्टी पलीद करना	1. To embarrass to the point of humiliation 2. To put someone in a miserable plight

मिट्टी बिगाड़ना	The last rites not to be performed properly
मिट्टी में मिलना	To be razed to the ground, To go to rack and ruin
मिट्टी में मिलाना	To destroy lock, stock and barrel
मिट्टी होना (किया कराया)	1. To come to grief 2. To go on the rocks
मिट्ठू बनना, अपने	To indulge in self-praise
मिट्ठू बनना, मियाँ	To speak flatteringly about oneself
मियाँ की जूती मियाँ के सिर	To beat somebody with his own stick
मियान में से निकल पड़ना	To be sudden and quick in quarrel, To go into a tantrum
मिर्चें-सी लगना	To be offended, To be visibly provoked
मिलना, अता-पता	To get a clue
मिलना, छुटकारा	To get release, To get rid of
मिलना, नतीजा	To get the result, To reap what one has sown
मिलाना, हाथ-से-हाथ	1. To be cooperative 2. To be cordial 3. To work shoulder to shoulder
मीठा मुँह कराना	To celebrate a happy occasion by offering sweetmeat
मीठी चुटकी	1. A pleasant pinch 2. A sweet joke

मीठी छुरी	1. A treacherous friend 2. A sugar-coated pill 3. A sweetened dagger
मीठी छुरी चलाना	To stab in the back
मीठी दवा देना	To gild the pill, To make a disagreeable task less offensive
मीठी मार	1. A left-handed compliment 2. Sarcastic remark 3. Slow torture
मीठी-मीठी बातों से पेट नहीं भरता	Fine words butter no parsnips
मीन-मेख निकालना	1. To carp, to criticise 2. To find fault with 3. To pick holes in
मीनाकारी छाँटना	To cross one's 't's and dot one's 'i's
मुँड़ जाना	To be fleeced, to be looted
मुँह, अपना-सा (लेकर) लौटना	1. To be humiliated 2. To look small 3. To return with downcast looks
मुँह उजला होना	To come out with flying colours
मुँह उतरना	To lose face
मुँह काला करना	1. To tarnish one's image 2. To disgrace oneself
मुँह की खाना	1. To be defeated 2. To be knocked out 3. To submit to humiliation 4. To suffer a severe reverse

मुँह की बात छीनना	To say what one was about to say, To take the words out of one's mouth
मुँह खुलना	To dare speak impertinently to
मुँह खोलना	To let out a secret, To reveal
मुँह चढ़ना	To take liberties with, To take to oneself unduly
मुँह चढ़ाना	To allow someone to take liberties
मुँह चलाना	1. To bite 2. To munch 3. To speak too much
मुँह चिढ़ाना	To jeer at, To mock
मुँह चुराना	To avoid being noticed
मुँह छिपाना	To hide one's face out of shame
मुँह टेढ़ा करना	To show contemptuous displeasure
मुँह ताकना	1. To look intently 2. To look to someone for some favour
मुँह तोड़ जवाब देना	To give a befitting reply, To give tit for tat, To jump down one's throat
मुँह दिखाना	To appear in public, To make an appearance, To show one's face

मुँह देखकर बात करना	To talk expediently
मुँह देखते रह जाना	To be taken aback, To look aghast
मुँह न देखना	To dislike (a person), To take an aversion to
मुँह न लगाना	To keep at bay
मुँह पकड़ना	To silence
मुँह पर कहना	To speak out to one's face
मुँह पर चढ़ना	To run in one's beard
मुँह पर ताला लगाना	To render one speechless
मुँह पर थूकना	To condemn, To cry shame upon, To insult, To treat with disrespect
मुँह पर नाक न होना	1. To be brazen-faced 2. To be shameless and immodest
मुँह पर हवाइयाँ उड़ना	1. To be out of countenance 2. To look blank
मुँह फुला लेना	1. To be in sulks 2. To put on a wry face
मुँह फेर लेना	To turn one's face away from, To turn the back on someone
मुँह फैलाना	To ask for too high a price, To be very greedy
मुँह बंद करना	To bribe, To give a sop, To grease one's palms
मुँह बनाना	To make/pull faces
मुँह बिचकाना	To grimace

मुँह बिगड़ना	1. To be displeased 2. To have a bad taste in the mouth
मुँह मारना	1. To behave treacherously 2. To practise infidelity
मुँह मियाँ मिट्ठू बनना, अपने	To blow one's own trumpet, To indulge in self-praise
मुँह मीठा करना	To celebrate an occasion by offering sweets
मुँह में खून लगना	To acquire a taste for wrong things, To develop liking for things depraved
मुँह में घी-शक्कर	May what you have uttered turn out to be true!
मुँह में पानी भर आना	1. Mouth beginning to water 2. To be impatiently keen to possess something 3. To lick one's chaps
मुँह में लगाम न होना	To be intemperate in speech, To be loose-tongued
मुँह मोड़ लेना	To run away from, To turn one's back upon
मुँह लगा	Cheeky, One allowed to take undue liberties
मुँह लगाना	To give undue lift to
मुँह लटकाना	To draw a long face, To sulk

मुँह सीधा न होना	To be out of element
मुँह सीना	To be tight-lipped, To silence
मुँह सी लेना	To choose to keep mum
मुँह सुजाना	To feel visibly annoyed, To sulk
मुँह से फूल झड़ना	To be extremely gentle in speech, To have honeyed lips
मुँह से निकल जाना (बात)	To escape one's lips (words) To divulge a secret unguardedly
मुँह से बात लेना	To stop another from speaking (by speaking oneself), To snatch words from another person's mouth
मुँह से लार टपकना	Mouth to water, To have a very strong desire to get a thing
मुँह हाथ टूटना	To be badly injured
मुँह-ही-मुँह में	To oneself (own)
मुकाबले की चोट होना	To meet one's match
मुट्ठी गरम करना	To bribe a person, To buy over, To grease one's palms
मुट्ठी गरम होना	To accept bribe, To be bribed
मुट्ठी ढीली होना	To shell out money
मुट्ठी में, जीत	Be sure to win, Victory to be in one's pocket

मुट्ठी में होना	1. To be in one's grip 2. To be under the control of 3. To twist somebody round one's little finger
मुलम्मा उतारना	To take the gilt off the ginger-bread
मुलम्मा चढ़ाना	To lend plausibility, To put up false show
मुश्किल में पड़ना	To be at a loss, To be in a fix, To be on the mat
मुस्तैद रहो	Keep your powder dry
मुसीबत खड़ी करना	To create a problem To land in trouble
मुसीबत मोल लेना	To invite trouble
मूँग, छाती पर (दलना)	1. To give one a hard time 2. To torment someone openly
मूँछें उखाड़ना	To crush (someone's) pride To give one a crushing defeat
मूँछें ऊँची करना	To feel proud of
मूँछें नीची होना	1. Lowering of one's pride 2. To be disgraced
मूँछें मुँडवाना	To admit defeat
मूँछों पर ताव देना (गर्व करना)	1. To express loftiness 2. To twirl one's whiskers out of boastfulness/pride
मूँड़ पाना	To be able to win (someone) over
मूँड़ मारना	1. To make strenuous efforts

	2. To tax one's brain
मूर्ख हर जगह दखल देते हैं	Fools rush in where angels fear to tread
मूसलचंद, दालभात में	1. An intruder 2. An unwelcome presence 3. Persona-non-grata 4. Wrong man in a wrong place
मेंढकी को जुकाम होना	To take to uncommon ways
मेरा-तेरा करना	Not to see beyond an inch of one's nose
मेरे मन कछु और है, साईं/कर्त्ता के कछु और	Man proposes, God disposes
मेल करना	To reconcile
मेल खाना	1. To accord (अनुकूल होना) 2. To be in harmony with 3. To correspond (अनुरूप होना)
मेला करना	To convene a large gathering, To hold a fair
मेला लगना	Large crowd to assemble
मैदान छोड़ देना	To flee, To run away from the battle-field, To show the white feather
मैदान जाना	To go to defecate
मैदान जीतना	To bear the palm, To score a victory, To win
मैदान मारना	1. To achieve success 2. To come out victorious

मैदान मार लेना	1. To carry the day 2. To score a victory
मैदान में उतरना	1. To be ready for a fight 2. To enter the arena 3. To jump into the fray 4. To pick up the gauntlet
मैदान में डटे रहना	To carry on the crusade, To stick to one's position
मैदान साफ करना	To clear all obstacles, To vanquish all adversaries
मैल रखना, मन में	To nurse a grudge
मैल लाना, मन में	To bear ill-will
मोम करना / होना	To melt, to move
मोम बनाना	To soften
मोरचा बाँधना	To take up strategic positions
मोरचा मारना	To achieve victory, To come out with flying colours
मोरचा लेना	To encounter an adversary
मौका हाथ लगना	To get a suitable opportunity
मौज उड़ाना	To kick up one's heels, To live high
मौज में आना	To be ecstatic, To get excited
मौत के घाट उतारना	To be done to death
मौत के मुँह में कूदना	To risk one's life
मौत सिर पर खेलना	Death hovering over one's head
मौत से खेलना	To risk one's life
मौनं स्वीकृति लक्षणम्	Silence is half consent
मौला, मस्त होना	To be carefree

म्याऊँ का ठौर	A dangerous place
म्याउँ म्याउँ करना	To speak in a subdued tone
म्यान में रहना	To be within one's limits
म्यान से निकलना	1. To be beside oneself with anger 2. To go beyond one's bounds

यथा नाम तथा गुण	As the name, so are the attributes
यथा राजा तथा प्रजा	As the king, so are the subjects
यदा-कदा	Occasionally, Sometimes, From time to time
यमपुरी पहुँचाना	To put to death
यश कमाना	1. To earn fame/name 2. To win fame
यश गाना	To eulogize, To sing the praises of
यश लूटना	1. To acquire fame 2. To usurp credit
यहाँ-वहाँ की बात	Evasive/irrelevant remarks
यों-त्यों करना	To curse

रंग आना	To be at one's best, To assume fullness
रंग उखड़ना	To lose charm, To lose influence
रंग उड़ जाना	1. To fade 2. To turn pale
रंग उतरना	To lose lustre, To lose wits
रंग चढ़ना	To be in full bloom
रंग जमना	1. To be in full swing 2. To establish one's dominance
रंग जमाना	To attain influential position
रंग टपकना	To be extraordinarily bright
रंग दिखाना	To exhibit various facets
रंग न जमना	1. Not to be able to deliver the goods 2. Not to be able to sell one's wares 3. To fall flat
रंग निकालना	To attain fullness

रंग पकड़ना	To be in full bloom
रंग पर आना	1. To be in full bloom 2. To be in full swing
रंग फीका करना	To take the shine out
रंग फीका पड़ना	To lose lustre
रंग बदलना	To change colours (for worse)
रंग बदलना (गिरगिट की तरह)	1. To change colours like chameleon 2. To turn cat in pan
रंग बिगड़ना	To lose one's image
रंग में भंग डालने वाला	Kill-joy
रंग में भंग होना	A fly in the ointment
रंग लगाना	Spoiling a gay occasion
रंग लाना	1. To bring about the needed change 2. To produce the desired effect
रंगा सियार, रंगीन मिजाज	A cunning fellow, Hot liver, Hypocrite
रंगे हाथ पकड़ना	To catch flat-footed To take by surprise
रंगे हाथ पकड़ा जाना	To be caught redhanded
रकम अटेरना	To grab money
रकम, चलती	A calculating mind
रकम मारना	To swallow money
रखना, आँख	To keep a vigil
रखना, दिल	To console
रखना, बात	To honour
रखना, मन में	Not to reveal,

	To keep in mind
रखना, मैल (मन में)	To nurse a grudge
रग, दुखती	Achilles' heel
रग पहचानना	To be thoroughly familiar, To know a person's inner nature
रग-रग में/से	1. All over 2. To the core
रगड़ा देना	To give a jolt
रगों में बिजली दौड़ना	To be electrified, To be greatly thrilled
रट लगाना	To go on insisting, To harp on the same tune
रफा-दफा करना	1. To cry quits 2. To dispose of 3. To hush up 4. To settle (a dispute)
रफू चक्कर हो जाना	To run away, To show a clean pair of heels, To slip away
रमता योगी बहता पानी	A wandering ascetic and flowing water are unfathomable
रमना, मन	1. To be distracted 2. To take delight in
रवाँ होना	To attain mastery To be perfect
रस्सियाँ तुड़ाकर भागना	1. To be impatient to have freedom 2. To strain at the leash

राई-भर	Very small quantity
राई रत्ती करके	1. Little by little 2. To the minutest details
राई से पर्वत/पहाड़ करना	To make a mountain of a mole-hill
राँगे को सब सोना मानते हैं, अपने	All one's geese are swans
राख डालना	To hush up
राख होना	To be razed to the ground
राग पूरना	To tell a long story
राग-रंग में रहना	To have fun all the time
राजा भोज कहाँ गंगू तेली, कहाँ	Not fit even to hold a candle to, To be very inferior
रात ढलना	Well past midnight
रात है तो प्रभात दूर नहीं	Every cloud has a silver lining
राम भरोसे छोड़ना	1. To leave in the lap of gods 2. To let things take their own course 3. To take one's chance
राम-राम करके	With great difficulty
राम-राम होना	To die
रावण की नाभि	Achilles' heel, Weak point
रास[१] आना	1. To agree, to suit (climate) 2. To prove favourable
रास[२] ढीली छोड़ना	To give a free hand
रास में लाना	To bring under one's control
रास्ता कटना	To cover the distance
रास्ता काटना	To cross one's path

रास्ता कतराना	1. To avoid going a particular way 2. To turn aside from road
रास्ता खुलना	The route to be opened
रास्ता देखना	To wait for
रास्ता पकड़ना	To set out on a particular path
रास्ता पकड़ो	Be off, Buzz off
रास्ता बताना	To get rid of, To show one the way
रास्ता साफ करना	To pave the way
रास्ते का काँटा	A hurdle on the way
रास्ते पर आना	1. To come round to one's views 2. To turn over a new leaf
रास्ते पर लाना	1. To bring one round to one's views 2. To bring to the right path 3. To win over
रास्ते लगना	To be suitably placed
राह दिखाना	1. To give one the lead 2. To set the pace
रिकार्ड तोड़ना	To break the record
रुख देखना	To see which way the wind blows
रुख बदलना	1. To change the aspect 2. To change the attitude 3. To switch over to the other side

रुख भाँपना	To feel the pulse of
रुख रखना	To continue to show favour
रुपया उड़ाना	To squander wealth
रुपया डूबना	To lose one's money
रुपया बनाना	To mint money
रुपया बहाना (पानी की तरह)	To burn the candle at both ends, To play ducks and drakes with one's money
रुपया मारना	To misappropriate
रुई की तरह धुनना	To give a severe thrashing
रेत की दीवार	A house of cards
रेत से तेल निकालना	1. To engage in fruitless enterprise 2. To milk the bull
रोग पालना/ लगा लेन.	To acquire a bad habit
रोटियाँ तोड़ना	1. To be a parasite, to be idle 2. To live as dependant
रोटियाँ लगना	To look prosperous
रोटियों से लगना	To begin earning one's livelihood
रोटी दाल चलाना	To keep wolf from the door, To make ends meet
रोटी दाल से खुश रहना	1. To be satisfied with one's lot 2. To have enough to live on
रोड़ा अटकाना	To place an obstacle, To put an impediment
रोना आना	To be on the point of weaping
रोना रोना, अपना	Everyone has one's own tale of woe

रोब गाँठना	To dominate, To overawe
रोब में आना	To be influenced, To be overawed
रो-रोकर काम करना	To work when driven hard
रोंगटे खड़े होना	Hair to stand on end
रौंदना, उम्मीदों को	Hopes to be shattered
रौला मचाना	To create an uproar

लंगर डालना / बैठाना	1. To cast anchor
	2. To serve free meal to all
लंगोट का कच्चा	1. A person of loose character
	2. One who has a weakness for sex
लंगोटिया यार	1. A bosom friend
	2. A childhood pal
लंबा करना	1. To knock one down
	2. To prolong
	3. To send off
लंबी तानना	To enjoy a deep carefree sleep
लंबी साँस लेना	1. To be filled with remorse
	2. To draw a deep breath
	3. To heave a sigh
लंबी-चौड़ी हाँकना	To talk big
लंबी हाँकना	1. To brag
	2. To talk boastfully
लंबे होना	To slip away
लकड़ियाँ देना	To perform the last rites
लकड़ी से सबको हाँकना, एक	1. To fail to show individual consideration

	2. To tar everybody with the same brush
लकड़ी होना	To grow lean and thin
लकीर का फकीर	1. Blind imitator, blind in faith
	2. Conventionalist, one of set outlook, status-quoist, traditionalist
लकीर पर चलना	To tread the beaten track
लकीर पीटना	1. To follow the tradition
	2. To repent
लगन लगना	1. To be devoted to
	2. To be in love with
	3. To be obsessed by
	4. To become fond of
	5. To have an intense interest in
लगना, आपस में	To be at logger-heads with each other
लगना, जी	To feel at home
लगना, पानी	To acclimatize oneself
लगना, बात	To feel offended by someone's words
लगना, मन	To be at ease
लगना, मुँह	To become cheeky
लगना, हवा	1. Exposure
	2. To be under the spell of
लगना, हाथ	To come by,
	To get
लगना, होड़	To vie with each other

लगाना, आँख / दिल	To fall in love, To lose one's heart to
लगाना, आग	To incite a quarrel
लगाना, इधर की उधर	To be a tale-bearer To indulge in rumour-mongering
लगाना, किनारे	To reach the destination
लगाना, ठिकाने	1. To dispose of 2. To put in right place
लगाना, नमक मिर्च	To aggravate the matter
लगाना, पार	To get over
लगाना, बात	To carry tales
लगाना बुझाना	1. To backbite 2. To be a continuing cause of trouble 3. To distort facts 4. To instigate
लगाना, मन	1. To apply one's mind 2. To concentrate
लगाना, मुँह	1. To allow one to take liberties 2. To be over-considerate 3. To have a liking
लगाना, मुँह में खून	To develop the inveterate habit of
लगाना, हाथ	1. To cooperate 2. To start work
लगाम लिए फिरना	To chase, intending to bring under restraint
लगाम कड़ी करना	To keep in check, To tighten one's hold

लगाम कसना	To be strict, To restrain
लगाम चढ़ाना	To bridle
लगाम ढीली करना	1. To allow latitude 2. To give a long rope 3. To loosen one's hold
लगाम देना	1. To check 2. To keep under restraint
लगाम, मुँह में (देना)	To bridle one's tongue, To talk with restraint
लगाम हाथ में लेना	To take control of, To take the reins in one's hand
लगी-लिपटी कहना	To speak with bias/ambiguously
लगे हाथों	1. Along with 2. At the same time 3. In addition to
लग्गा लगना	1. To be attached 2. To start
लग्गा लगाना	1. To begin 2. To form an attachment
लटकना, अधर में	To be in suspense, To hang in fire
लटकना, मुँह	Face fell, To pull a long face
लटकना, सूली पर जान	To pass very anxious moments
लट्टू हो जाना	To be enamoured of, To fall in love, To lose one's heart to
लट्टू होना (किसी पर)	1. To be captivated by

	2. To be enthusiastic about 3. To fall for 4. To be fascinated (by somebody) 5. To be infatuated with
लट्ठ लिए फिरना, अक्ल के पीछे	1. To go on committing one foolish act after another 2. To take leave of one's senses
लट्ठ लिए फिरना, किसी के पीछे	To have it in for (someone)
लड़ना, आँखें	Exchange of amorous glances, To look lovingly
लड़ना, किस्मत	To be in for luck
लड़ाई की जड़	Apple of discord, Bone of contention
लड़ाई के बीज बोना	To sow dragon's teeth
लड़ाई ठानना	To fall out
लड़ाई बंद कर देना	1. To cease hostilities 2. To lay down arms
लड़ाई मोल लेना	To pick up quarrel
लड़ाई लेना	To join battle
लड़ाना, लाड़	To pamper
लड्डू खिलाना	To bribe a person
लड्डू बँटना	To have festivities
लड्डू बाँटना	To celebrate some happy occasion
लडडू, मन के (खाना)	To build castles in the air
लड्डू मिलना	To get something worthwhile
लत्ते ले डालना	To reprimand severely
लपेट में आना	To fall into the grip of
लब खोलना	To speak out one's mind

लब पर आना	To be on the tip of one's tongue
लबड़-धौंधौं मचाना	To create unnecessary confusion
लल्लो-चप्पो करना	To flatter, To pay court to
लहर आना	1. To have a sudden stroke of luck 2. To suffer a fit
लहर लेना	To enjoy oneself
लहू उतरना	To become bloodshot
लहू का घूँट पीना	To suppress anger
लहू का प्यासा	Extremely angry
लहू चूसना/ पीना	To exploit up to the hilt
लहू-पसीना एक करना	To toil by the sweat of one's brow
लहू पी-पीकर रह जाना	1. To suppress one's rage 2. To worry
लहू में हाथ रंगना	To stain one's hands with the blood of
लहू सफेद होना	To grow inhumane
लाँग खुलना	1. To be agitated 2. To become nervous
लाख का घर खाक होना	To be reduced from plenty to penury
लाख टके की बात	An invaluable remark
लाख रुपए की बात	A strikingly remarkable utterance
लाखों में खेलना	To wallow in riches
लाग-लपेट न रखना	To call a spade a spade, To speak frankly

लाठी एक (से हाँकना)	To tar everybody with the same brush
लाठी, जिसकी (उसकी भैंस)	Might is right
लात खाना	To be spurned
लात मारना	To spurn
लात मारना, लज्जा को	To shed all sense of shame
लातों के भूत बातों से नहीं मानते	Honey is not made for the ass's mouth (Persuasion will not persuade fools)
लानत भेजना	To condemn, to curse
लार टपकना	To crave for something pleasant to eat,
	To have an uncontrollable desire for
लालच बुरी बला है	Avarice is the root of all evils
	Greed is a great curse
लाल[१] पड़ना/होना	1. To flush
	2. To turn red with rage
लाल-पीला होना	1. To be beside oneself with rage
	2. To be infuriated, to look black
लाल रहना	To flourish
लाल आँखें दिखाना	To frown,
	To give vent to one's anger
लाल आँखें निकालना	To fly into a fit of rage
लाल[२] धरती के	The sons of the soil
लाल लालों का	Dearest
लाले पड़ना, जान के	1. Life to be in jeopardy

	2. To be in a hopeless state
लाश-पर-लाश गिरना	To die in quick succession
लिखत में लाना	To put down in black and white
लीक पर चलना	To follow the beaten track
लीक पीटना	To follow blindly
लीक से बेलीक चलना	1. To blaze a trail 2. To deviate from the usual practice 3. To go astray
लीपना	To gloss over one's failure etc.
लीप-पोत कर बराबर करना	To ruin completely
लीपा-पोती करना	1. To offer excuse for 2. To put a gloss upon 3. To whitewash
लुटना, सुहाग	To be reduced to widowhood
लुटिया डुबोना	To spell ruination
लुटिया डूबना	To be ruined
लू-लू बनना	To be a fool
ले उड़ना	1. To abduct 2. To kidnap
ले-दे करके	All told
ले-दे करना	To bargain
ले बैठना	To be the cause of one's ruination
ले रखना	To lay by
ले रहना	To manage to earn
लेना, आड़े हाथों	1. To give someone a piece of one's mind 2. To take someone to task

लेना एक न देना दो	1. For no purpose at all 2. To have no concern whatsoever 3. To have nothing to gain or lose
लेने के देने पड़ना	1. To be drawn into an unexpected difficulty 2. To go out for wool and come home shorn 3. To have the tables turned upon oneself
लेने में, न देने में	To have nothing to do with anything
लोंदा, मिट्टी का	A worthless fellow
लोट-पोट होना	1. To be restless 2. To burst into peals of laughter
लोटा, बेपेंदे का	A spineless person
लोहा बजाना	To be engaged in fighting
लोहा मानना	1. To acknowledge some one's superiority 2. To acknowledge the calibre of
लोहा लेना	To cross swords with, To wage war
लोहे के चने चबाना	1. To crack the hard nut 2. To undertake an uphill task
लोहे को लोहा काटता है	Diamond cuts diamond
लौ लगाना	To concentrate on

व

वचन देना	To undertake
वचन निभाना	To keep one's promise
वज्र गिरना	A bolt from the blue
वार करो पर सही वक्त पर	Strike the iron when it is hot
वारे-न्यारे करना	1. To decide finally 2. To mint money 3. To settle the matter once for all
वारे-न्यारे होना	To become rich
वास्ता पड़ना	1. To exist with 2. To have to deal with
वास्ता रखना	To have to do with
विद्वान् का बेटा मूर्ख हो सकता है	Good cow may have an ill calf
विद्वान व्यक्ति	A man of parts
विधि की विडंबना	Irony of fate
विपत पड़े जो कर गहे, सोई साँचो मीत	A friend in need is a friend indeed
विष घोलना	1. To disturb someone's life 2. To poison the happiness of
विषस्य विषमौषधम्	Like cures like diseases
वेष बदलना/रखना	To disguise
व्यर्थ का काम करना	To beat the air

शक्ल देखते रह जाना	To gaze in astonishment
शक्ल से मोमन, करतूत से काफिर	Wolf in lamb's clothing
शगूफा छोड़ना	To kick up a row To let off a squib
शतरंज का मोहरा	Cat's paw, Person used as a tool by another
शर्म घोलकर पी जाना	To have lost all sense of shame
शह देना	1. To encourage 2. To incite
शह पाना	1. To be encouraged by 2. To give someone rope
शहद की छुरी	A honey-tongued crook
शहद लगाकर चाटना	1. To be of no avail 2. To bother much for a vain thing 3. To treasure something worthless
शहीदों में नाम लिखाना	To be a sham martyr
शांत होना	To be silenced

शान झाड़ना/मारना	To make a great display
शान बघारना	To boast, To brag, To give oneself airs
शान में बट्टा लगना	1. A fair name to be tarnished 2. To be derogatory to one's dignity
शाम-सुबह करना	To evade/shirk
शामत आना	To be in for trouble
शामत सिर पर खेलना/का मारा	Struck by misfortune
शिकन न पड़ना (चेहरे पर)	To remain unruffled
शिकार करना, एक पत्थर से	To kill two birds with one stone
शिकार होना	To fall prey
शीशे में देखना, अपना मुँह	To examine oneself in a mirror
शेख-चिल्ली	1. Starry-eyed 2. Impractical
शेखी किरकिरी होना	To be humiliated
शेखी बघारना/मारना/हाँकना	To boast, to brag, To give oneself airs
शेर की खाल में गधा	A fool who apes the wise man, An ass in lion's skin
शेर की माँद में पैर रखना	To do a risky job, To venture a dangerous undertaking
शेर के मुँह में जाना	To face a hazard
शेर होना	1. To be brave 2. To become cheeky
शैतान की आँत	To let off a squib, A tale that knows no end
शोशा छोड़ना	To spread a false story

श्रीगणेश अच्छा हो तो काम हुआ समझो

1. The first blow is half the battle
2. Well begun is half done

श्री गणेश करना

1. To begin any operation
2. To break ground
3. To break the ice
4. To commence operations
5. To make a start by getting over initial difficulties
6. To ring up the curtain

संकट का साथी	A friend in need
संकट की घड़ी	Critical hour
संदेह दूर करना	To clear the air
सकते की हालत होना	State of being confounded
सकते में आना	To be astounded
सत निकालना	Skim the cream off, Take the best part of
सत निचोड़ लेना	Squeeze out the most significant property of a thing
सत्तू बाँधकर पीछे पड़ना	To pursue (a goal) with single-minded devotion
सत्तू सानना	To mince matters
सनक सवार होना	To be obsessed by a craze
सनीचर आना	Misfortune to befall
सनीचर पाँव में (होना)	To be constantly on the move
सन्नाटा खींचना	To become quite silent
सन्नाटा छाना	Dead silence
सन्नाटे में आना	To be stupefied
सपाटा मारना, से	To rush

सफाई जताना	To demonstrate one's blamelessness, To vindicate
सफाई देना	1. To clarify 2. To defend 3. To justify
सफाया करना	To wipe out completely
सबसे भली चुप, सबसे भला चुप रहना	Silence is golden
सबक लेना	To learn a lesson (from an experience)
सब्ज बाग दिखाना	1. To arouse high hopes/ promises (in vain) 2. To lead the person up the garden path 3. To mislead
सब्र का फल मीठा होता है	Slow and steady wins the race
समझ पर पत्थर पड़ना	To lose one's wits
समझ से परे	Beyond one's ken
समय, आड़े	Rainy day, Time of distress
समय काटना	To while away time
समय की बात	Matter of chance
समय चूकना	To miss an opportunity
समाँ बँधना	A mood to be created
समाँ बाँधना	To keep the audience spell-bound
समाना, फूले न	Joy knowing no bounds, Not to be able to contain oneself with joy

सर करना	To overpower
सर मुँड़ाते ही ओले पड़ना	Misfortune to befall at the very outset
सर होना	To win
सराय का कुत्ता	A shameless opportunist
सलाम करना	1. To acknowledge the superiority of
	2. To refrain from
	3. To salute
सलाम दूर से (करना)	To avoid meeting,
	To keep some one at an arm's length
सवार होना, छाती पर	To keep on pestering
सवार होना, सिर पर	To behave insolently
सस्ता लगना	To be available cheaply,
	To look cheap
सस्ते छूटना	To have to spend less than usual
सहलाना, तलवे	To indulge in servile flattery,
	To lick the feet of
सही करना	1. To adjust
	2. To attest
	3. To endorse
	4. To verify
साँच को आँच नहीं	Truth knows no fear
साँचे में ढले, एक ही	Cast in the same mould,
	Identical
साँड़ की तरह घूमना	To roam about freely
साँप, आस्तीन का	A snake in the grass

साँप कलेजे पर लोटना	To come under the spell of green-eyed god
साँप के बिल में हाथ डालना	To invite danger
साँप को दूध पिलाना	To feed the ungrateful
साँप, दो मुहाँ	1. A very dangerous person 2. Two-headed dragon
साँप-न्यौले का बैर	Eternal enmity
साँप पालना	To nurture a viper
साँप मर जाए लाठी न टूटे	To achieve one's objective without suffering any loss
साँप सूँघ जाना	To cast a chill over
साँप से खेलना	To play a dangerous game
साँस जब तक, तब तक आस	Hope sustains life While there is life, there's hope
साँस ठंडी (भरना) / लेना	To heave a sigh of relief
साख उठ जाना	To lose credibility
साख में बट्टा लगना	Goodwill to be lost
सागपात समझना	To treat contemptuously
सात-पाँच करना	To make lame excuses, To raise unnecessary queries
सात परदों में रखना	To keep away from all eyes
सातों वचन	Marriage vows
साथ निभाना	To stand by through thick and thin
साधना/साफ करना, हाथ	1. To acquire a skill 2. To practise
साफ करना, जूते	To play sycophant
साफ जवाब देना	1. To declare the case hopeless 2. To give a curt reply

साफ निकल जाना	To escape unhurt
साफ हिसाब	To clear off
साफ होना	1. To be cleaned 2. To be swept bare, to be devastated by epidemic
साया उठ जाना	1. To be bereft of a protective hand 2. To be ophaned
साया डालना	To show favour
साया न पड़ने देना	To keep scrupulously aloof from someone
साया पड़ना	To come under the influence of
साये में पलना	To be brought up under the care/patronage of
साये में रहना	To live under care
साये से दूर रहना	To keep away even from the shadow of
सारी दीखै जात आधी लीजै बाँट	Better give the wool than the whole sheep
सावन के अंधे को हरा-ही-हरा दिखता है	Everything looks yellow to a jaundiced eye
सावन हरे न भादो सूखे	Continually unaffected by external changes
सिंदूर डालना / भरना, माँग में	To marry (a woman)
सिंदूर पोंछना	To become a widow
सिकोड़ना, नाक-भौं	To show displeasure/disliking
सिक्का जमना	1. To attain distinction 2. To establish one's domination/superiority

	3. To make one's mark
सिक्का मानना	To concede the influence of
सिट्टी-पिट्टी भूल जाना/गुम होना	1. To be dumb-founded
	2. To be in a blue funk
	3. To be stunned
सितम करना / ढाना	1. To cast a spell on
	2. To cause havoc
	3. To charm
	4. To enchant
सितम टूटना	1. An outrage
	2. To be charmed (by the bewitching beauty of a woman)
सितारा गर्दिश में होना	Down on one's luck
सितारा चमकना, किस्मत का	To be lucky, to be successful, To hit the jackpot
सितारा बुलंद होना	The star to be in the ascendant
सिप्पा जमाना	1. To lay the ground
	2. To succeed
सिप्पा भिड़ाना/मारना	1. To achieve a goal
	2. To deploy all means to achieve one's objective
	3. To manoeuvre
सिफारिशी टट्टू	1. One who obtains a post not by dint of his merit but through the influence of others
	2. A recommendee
सिर आँखों पर / से	1. Most willingly

	2. To offer a place of honour
	3. To treat most affectionately and cordially
सिर उठाना	To rebel, to rise in revolt
सिर उड़ा देना / कलम करना	To behead,
	To put to death
सिर ओखली में देना	To be ready to face all concequences,
	To invite trouble
सिर का बवाल	Headache
सिर के बल	1. Headlong
	2. With due deference
	3. With great pleasure
सिर के बाल नोंच डालना	To tear one's hair in despair
सिर खाना	To pester
सिर खुजाना	To court punishment
सिर चढ़ना	1. To become cheeky,
	2. To take much lift
	3. To take too much liberty
सिर चढ़ाना	1. To give undue liberty
	2. To spoil someone (a child) by over-indulgence
सिर चीरना	To insist on having one's own way
सिर झुकना	To feel ashamed
सिर झुकाना / झुका लेना	1. To bow, to be submissive
	2. To hang one's head in shame
सिर टकराना	1. To strike one's head against

	2. To subject oneself to a great deal of mental exercise
सिर थोपना	1. To impose upon
	2. To place the responsibility on someone for something
सिर धुनना	To lament, to mourn, to weep
सिर न पैर	Absurd, baseless, irrelevent
सिर नीचा होना	To be disgraced, To feel ashamed
सिर पटकना	To make frantic efforts, To wail
सिर पर आ जाना	To approach very near, To be quite at hand
सिर पर आसमान उठाना	1. To play havoc
	2. To raise a great clamour
सिर पर उठाना	To create confusion
सिर पर कफन बाँधना	To be ready to face death, To take a risk of one's life
सिर पर कयामत करना	To cause an uproar, To create havoc
सिर पर कयामत होना/टूटना	To be in hot waters, A calamity to befall
सिर पर खड़ा होना	To hang hover around, To pester by being present
सिर पर चढ़ना	To behave rudely, to harass
सिर पर पाँव रखकर भागना	To take to one s heels
सिर पर बनना	To be in great trouble
सिर पर लेना	1. To own,
	2. To take responsibility

सिर पर सवार होना	1. To bully 2. To obsess
सिर पर साया होना	To be under the protection of, To have someone over as a well-wisher
सिर पर सेहरा बाँधना	1. To earn distinction 2. To have a feather in one's cap 3. To plume upon 4. To win laurels
सिर पर हाथ फेरना	To console
सिर पर हाथ रखना	To provide protection to
सिर फिरना	1. To go to one's head 2. To run amuck 3. To turn one's head
सिर मढ़ना	1. To heap blame on someone 2. To lay blame on some one 3. To pass the buck to
सिर मारना	To take great pains
सिर मुँड़ाते ही ओले पड़ना	Ill-luck to overtake at the very outset
सिर से पानी ऊपर होना/गुजरना	1. To be intolerable 2. To cross the limit of tolerance
सिर से पैर तक आग लगना	To burn with jealousy
सिर से बला टालना	To get rid of a botheration
सिर हिलाना	To nod the head (in agreement or disagreement)
सिर होना	To annoy, to pester
सींग कटाकर बछड़ों में मिलना	Ripe age, raw ways
सींग निकलना	1. To attain maturity

	2. To take to strange ways
सींग समाना	To find shelter
सीख देना	To teach a lesson
सीख लेना	To draw a lesson
सीढ़ी खींच लेना, नीचे से	To leave someone in mid-air
सीढ़ी चढ़ना, सोने की	To die after becoming great grand-father
सीधा करना	1. To correct
	2. To set right
	3. To straighten
सीधी आँख से देखना	To adopt a favourable attitude towards someone
सीधे मुँह बात न करना/ नहीं बोलना	Not to talk with due courtesy, To behave condescendingly
सी न करना	Not to utter a painful sound
सीना तानकर चलना	To behave pretentiously,
	To walk with head held high
सीना तानकर रखना	To carry oneself defiantly
सीने पर पत्थर रख लेना	1. To repress sorrow
	2. To suppress anguish quietly
सीने से लगाकर रखना	To show all affection
सुंदर वही जो सुंदर काम करे	Handsome is that handsome does
सुख की नींद सोना	1. To enjoy a sound sleep
	2. To have peace of mind
	3. To lead a carefree life
सुख के साथ दुःख लगा है	Roses have thorns
सुख देखना	To live a happy and comfortable life

सुख लूटना	To enjoy to one's fill
सुध करना / रखना / लेना	1. To remember 2. To enquire after 3. To take care of
सुध दिलाना	To remind
सुध-बुध मारी जाना	To lose one's wits
सुनाना, खरी-खोटी	To take one to task
सुनाना जली-कटी	1. To give one a bit of one's mind 2. To utter harsh words
सुनी-अनसुनी करना/कर देना	Not to pay any heed, To turn a deaf ear
सुनी-सुनाई (बात)	Hearsay
सुबह-शाम करना	To put off on some pretext or the other, To procrastinate
सुरखाब का पर होना	To be extraordinarily intelligent
सुर-से-सुर मिलाना	To chime in
सुराग लगाना	To find a clue
सुराग हाथ लगना	To get a clue
सुलह हो जाना	To make it up
सुहागा, सोने में	One excellence superimposed over another
सूँघ जाना, साँप	To be stunned
सूंई का फावड़ा बना देना	To make a mountain of a mole hill
सूंई के नाके में से ऊँट निकालना	1. To perform an impossible feat 2. To try to do miracles

	3. To try to pass a camel through the eye of a needle
सूख जाना, खून	To be horror-stricken, To freeze one's blood
सूखा जवाब	A blunt reply, a flat refusal
सूखी सुनाना	To rebuke
सूझ-बूझ से काम लेना	To act imaginatively
सूना करना	To destroy
सूना लगना	To feel lonely
सूरज को दीपक दिखाना	1. To introduce a well known person 2. To need no introduction
सूरज पर थूकना	To debase oneself by accusing an innocent person
सूरत दिखाना	To appear, to show up, to turn up
सूरत न निकलना	To be left with no alternative
सूरत नजर आना	A solution to appear in sight
सूरत बनना	Things to take a concrete shape
सूरत बिगड़ना	To deface
सूरत से बेजार होना	To be fed up
सूरत (किस सूरत) से?	With what show of honour?
सूर्य को दीपक दिखाना	1. To introduce a well known person 2. To need no introduction
सूली पर टँगना, जान	To be overanxious
सेंकना, आँखें	To feast one's eyes
सेंकना, हाथ	To take undue advantage of another's suffering

सेज, काँटों की	Bed of thorns
सेज, फूलों की	Bed of roses
सेर को सवा सेर मिलना	1. To catch a Tartar 2. To come across one who is more than a match
सेवा करना	1. To attend 2. To look after
सेवा बजाना	To perform a service
सेहरा बँधना	1. To be married 2. To get credit
सेहरा बाँधना	1. To get married 2. To give credit for
सोंठ हो जाना	To remain silent
सोती भिड़ को न जगाना	1. Let sleeping dogs lie 2. Not to rake up the controversial issue
सोने का घर मिट्टी करना	To squander one's wealth
सौ की सीधी बात कहना	The long and short of a matter
सौ-सौ घड़े पानी पड़ना	To be highly embarrassed
सौ हाथ का कलेजा होना	To be vastly generous
स्यापा खत्म होना	Ending of an unpleasant episode
स्याह सफेद करना	To make or mar
स्याह सफेद का मालिक	Undisputed master
स्याही पोतना, चेहरे पर	To defame
स्वान्तः सुखाय (कार्य)	1. Labour of love 2. Work that one enjoys doing

हँड़िया चढ़ना	To enjoy a lucky spell, To keep the pot boiling
हँड़िया पकना	A scheme to be on the anvil
हंस कभी कीचड़ नहीं खाता	1. A really noble heart will never disgrace oneself 2. The eagle does not hawk at flies
हँसकर बात उड़ाना	To dismiss as unimportant, To laugh away
हँसते-हँसते मुसीबत झेलना	To pass difficult time cheerfully
हँसते-हँसते पेट में बल पड़ जाना	To burst into peals of laughter
हँसते-हँसते लोट-पोट हो जाना	To go on laughting till one's sides begin to ache, To laugh into cramps
हँसी उड़ना	To be ridiculed
हँसी उड़ाना / टालना	To laugh at, to ridicule
हँसी-ठट्ठा समझना	To set no store by, To take as a child's play, To think little of
हँसी में उड़ाना	To laugh away.

	To laugh off
हँसी में खाँसी	To carry a joke too far,
	To descend from words to blows
हँसी समझना	To take lightly,
	To treat as a joke
हक अदा करना	1. To discharge one's obligation
	2. To do one's duty
	3. To pay a debt
हक दबाना	To deprive one of one's right
हक में काँटे बोना	1. To create obstacles for someone
	2. To do an evil turn to
हकीकत खुलना	1. The cat is out of the bag
	2. The truth has come out
हक्का-बक्का रह जाना	To be taken aback
हजम करना	To digest, to embezzle
हजम होना	To be assimilated
हजामत बनाना	To dupe, to fleece
हजार रंग बदलना	To be very fickle,
	To change colours like chameleon
हटना, बात से	To go back on one's words
हड़बड़ी सवार होना	To be obsessed by undue haste
हड़ लगे न फिटकरी, रंग चौखा होना	To achieve the desirable result without much effort and expense
हड्डियाँ निकलना	To be reduced to a skeleton
हड्डी-पसली एक कर देना	To give one a good drubbing/ thrashing

हड्डी, पुरानी	A tough old fellow
हत्थे चढ़ना/पड़ना	To fall into the clutches of
हत्थे मारना	To haul down quickly
हत्थे लगना	To happen to meet by chance
हत्थे से उखड़ना	To be derailed
हत्या टलना	To get rid of an affliction
हत्या मोल लेना	To invite trouble
हत्या सिर लेना	To involve oneself in serious trouble
हथकंडे दिखाना	1. To show one's tactics 2. To take recourse to manoeuvring
हथियार डाल देना	1. To admit defeat 2. To lay down one's arms 3. To surrender
हथेली खुजलाना	An omen for money to flow in
हथेली पर जान लेकर घूमना	To expose one's life to danger
हथेली पर जान/सिर रखना	To risk one's life
हथेली पर सरसों जमाना	1. To accomplish a feat within too short a time 2. To expect results prematurely 3. To perform wonders
हरफन मौला हरफन अधूरा	Jack of all trades and master of none
हर बूँद मोती नहीं बनती	Not every mind will answer equally
हर लेना, पीड़ा	To relieve one of one's pain
हर लेना, मन	To captivate the heart
हरा मन (होना)	1. To be delighted, to be overjoyed

	2. To feel refreshed
हराम, जीना	To make one's life miserable
हराम करना (होना), नींद	To disturb one's sleep
हरी झंडी दिखाना	To give clearance, To give green signal To give line clear
हरी-हरी सूझना	1. To be unduly optimistic 2. To look always on the bright side of things
हरे-हरे बाग दिखाना	To give false hopes
हलक के नीचे न उतरना	Not to go down one's throat, To be unable to accept
हलक से नीचे उतरना	1. To be convinced 2. To accept
हलका करना	1. To abate (price) 2. To lighten
हलका होना, मन	To feel light To unburden one's heart
हलकी पड़ जाना, बात	Words to lose their weight
हलचल डालना	To strike terror
हलचल मचाना	To create panic/stir
हलदी चढ़ाना	To give a cosmetic-bride
हलदी लगाकर बैठना	1. To do nothing 2. To sit idle
हलदी लगे न फिटकरी	To invest nothing, to gain everything
हलवा करना	To thrash soundly
हलवा-मांडा	Loaves and fishes
हलवा समझना	To think easy to perform

हलाल की कमाई करना	Well-begotten earning
हवा उड़ना	1. News to go round 2. Rumour to be set afloat
हवा उड़ाना	To give currency to a rumour
हवा कर देना	To cause to evaporate into thin air
हवा का रुख देखना / पहचानना	1. To keep one's ear to the ground 2. To see the prevailing trends 3. To see which way the wind blows
हवा के घोड़े पर सवार	To be in a frantic hurry
हवा के रुख चलना	To move with the times
हवा देखा करना	To keep an eye on the situation
हवा देना	To encourage, to spur
हवा न लगने देना	2. To keep top secret 1. Not to let a thing be exposed
हवा निकल जाना	1. To become humble, after having once been arrogant and boastful 2. To cease boasting and assuming a lower tone 3. To feel small 4. To get deflated
हवा निकालना	1. To deflate 2. To lower one's pride 3. To take one down a button-hole
हवा पर होना	To be on one's high horse

हवा फाँककर रहना	To starve
हवा बदलना	1. Things to change 2. To go to some other place for change of climate
हवा बाँधकर चलना	To go against the wind
हवा बाँधना	1. To brag 2. To earn name
हवा बिगड़ना	1. Situation to change entirely for the worse 2. To be in a tight corner
हवा लगना	1. To be influenced by 2. To catch the ways of
हवा से बातें करना	1. To drive/fly/run at a terrific speed 2. To talk in the air
हवा से लड़ना	1. To be out to pick up a quarrel 2. To indulge in shadow-boxing
हवा हो जाना	1. To disappear 2. To evaporate into thin air
हवाइयाँ उड़ना, मुँह पर	1. Face to lose all lustre 2. To appear non-plussed 3. To be terror-struck
हवाई किले बनाना	To build castles in the air To live in the make-believe world
हवास खो बैठना	To lose one's wits
हवास गुम होना	To be non-plussed

हवास ठिकाने होना	To be in one's right mind
हस्ती मिटाना	To wipe out one's being
हस्ती होना, बड़ी	1. To be a big gun 2. To be a big personage 3. To grow too big for one's boots
हाँ जी, हाँ जी करना	1. To be a yes man 2. To keep on flattering
हाँड़ी गरम होना	To pocket bribe
हाँड़ी पकना	To hatch a plot
हाँड़ी फूटना	Revealing hitherto hidden matters
हाँड़ी बार-बार नहीं चढ़ती, काठ की	Once a traitor always a traitor
हाँ में हाँ मिलाना	1. To agree 2. To ditto 3. To be a yes-man
हा खाना, हा-हा खाना	To entreat cringingly
हाजत रफा करना	To fulfil one's requirement
हाजिरी देना	To attend
हाजिरी बजाना	To dance attendence on
हाड़ पेलना	To put in extremely hard labour
हाथ आजमाना	To try one's hand
हाथ आना	1. To come under control 2. To gain
हाथ उठाना	To attack, To beat
हाथ कट जाना	To be helpless
हाथ कटा लेना/कटाना	1. To be rendered helpless

	2. To deprive oneself of freedom of action
हाथ कमर पर रखना	To be weak
हाथ का मैल (धन)	To be of no consequence
हाथ की कठपुतली	A puppet in the hands of
हाथ की लकीर	One's fate
हाथ की सफ़ाई	Manual skill
हाथ के तोते उड़ जाना	To be petrified
हाथ के नीचे आना	To fall into the clutches of
हाथ खाली जाना	1. To go empty-handed 2. To miss the target/mark
हाथ खाली न होना	Hands to be full, To be busy
हाथ खाली होना	1. To be penniless 2. To have nothing to do
हाथ खींच लेना	1. To cease to have interest 2. To sever connection with 3. To wash one's hands off 4. To withdraw support
हाथ खुजलाना	1. To feel like beating someone 2. A happy augury for money to come in soon
हाथ खुलना	1. One given to hitting readily 2. To play ducks and drakes with money 3. To spend lavishly
हाथ खून से रंगे होना	To have committed murder
हाथ गरम होना	To accept bribe
हाथ चलाना / छोड़ना	To hit,

	To strike
हाथ जमना	1. To administer slap
	2. To attain mastery in
हाथ जमाना	1. To acquire perfection
	2. To give a blow, to slap
हाथ झाड़ना	1. To show that one has no money on his person
	2. To strike
हाथ डालना	1. To meddle
	2. To undertake a work
	3. To violate the modesty (physically)
हाथ तंग होना	To be hard up,
	To be tight (financially)
हाथ दबना	1. To be in hot waters
	2. To be in the grip of a crisis
हाथ दिखाना	1. To have one's palm read by an astrologer
	2. To show one's skill
	3. To show proof of one's efficacy
हाथ देना	1. To give signal
	2. To lend a helping hand
हाथ धरना	To support
हाथ धोकर पीछे पड़ना	1. To pursue obsessively
	2. To pursue with a vengeance
हाथ धो बैठना	To wash one's hands off
हाथ न रखने देना	To allow no quarter whatsoever
हाथ पकड़ना	1. To accept a woman as a spouse

	2. To look after
	3. To obstruct
	4. To provide support
हाथ पर सरसों जमाना	To show one's promptness
हाथ-पर-हाथ धरे बैठना	To sit idly all the time
हाथ-पर-हाथ मारना	1. To promise,
	2. To shake hands
हाथ पसारे जाना	To go to the other world empty-handed
हाथ पाँव फूलना	To be extremely nervous
हाथ पीले करना	To marry off a daughter
हाथ-पैर चलाना	To exert for earning livelihood
हाथ-पैर जोड़ना/चूमना	To be on one's knees,
	To make humble entreaties
हाथ-पैर ठंडे हो जाना	To pass away
हाथ-पैर फूल जाना	To be nervous, to be stunned
हाथ-पैर मारना	To try one's level best
हाथ फेरना	1. To caress,
	2. To rob
हाथ फैलाना	To extend a needy hand for help
हाथ बँटाना	1. To cooperate, extend cooperation
	2. To lend a helping hand
हाथ बचाना	To defend oneself against a blow,
	To protect oneself
हाथ बाँधे खड़े रहना	To be at one's beck and call
हाथ बिकना (किसी के)	1. To be a slave to

	2. To be in utter subservience
हाथ बैठ जाना	To have acquired a proficiency
हाथ भर का कलेजा होना	1. To be wildly delighted 2. To have tremendous courage
हाथ भर की जबान होना	To be insolently outspoken
हाथ मँजना	To attain mastery
हाथ मजबूत करना	To strengthen one's hands
हाथ मलना	To wring one's hands in despair/sorrow
हाथ मारना	1. To acquire control over 2. To embezzle 3. To lay hands on 4. To pilfer
हाथ में खुजली होना	1. To feel like beating someone 2. An omen for monetary gain
हाथ में दिल रखना	To wear one's heart on one's sleeve
हाथ में नकेल होना	To be under the control of
हाथ में मेहँदी लगी होना	1. To be absolutely idle 2. To be incapable of taking necessary action.
हाथ में लगाम होना	1. To control 2. To hold the reins of
हाथ रंगना	1. To stain one's hand with 2. To take bribe
हाथ रखना	To support
हाथ लगना	1. To come by 2. To lay hands on

हाथ लगाना	1. To beat 2. To commence work 3. To strike
हाथ समेटना / सिकोड़ना	1. To refrain from 2. To restrain one's hands from 3. To withdraw support
हाथ साफ करना	To plunder, to pilfer
हाथ सिर पर रखना	1. To patronize 2. To swear by one's life 3. To take one under protection
हाथ से जाना	To get out of hand
हाथ से ताली नहीं बजती, एक	It takes two to make a quarrel
हाथ से बेहाथ होना	To get out of control
हाथ होना	To have a hand
हाथापाई (मुठभेड़)	Hand to hand fight
हाथापाई पर उतरना	To come to blows
हाथी के दाँत खाने के और दिखाने के और	All that glitters is not gold
हाथी के पाँव में सबका पाँव	When God is worshipped, all gods are worshipped
हाथी झूलना, घर पर	To be very prosperous
हाथी निकल गया, पूँछ रह गई	To have completed the entire task, save the fractional, To break the neck of the task
हाथों की कठपुतली	1. A puppet in the hands of 2. To dance to the tune of
हाथों के तोते उड़ जाना	To become utterly confused
हाथों में खेलना	To play in the hands of
हाथों, रंगे (पकड़ा जाना)	To be caught red-handed

हाथों लेना	To give a warm reception
हाथों लेना, आड़े	To take one to task
हाथों-हाथ ले जाना	1. To carry away without losing time 2. To snatch away
हाथों-हाथ ले लेना	1. To receive cordially 2. To receive one with all respect
हाय लेना	To invite the curse of
हाय-हाय मचाना	Pandemonium to prevail
हार का मुँह देखना	To suffer defeat
हार मानना	To lower one's sail, To throw up the sponge
हालत पतली होना	1. To be in a miserable state 2. To be in an indifferent state of health 3. To be out of funds
हावी होना	To dominate, To get the better of
हिम्मत बँधाना	To buck up
हिम्मत से काम लेना	To handle boldly, To have the heart
हिम्मत हारना	To lose heart
हिरन हो जाना	To take to one's heels, To vanish
हिल जाना, आसन	1. One's seat to become wobbly 2. One's position to be put in jeopardy/become shaky
हिसाब चुकता करना	To clear off account

हिसाब चुकाना	To square accounts with
हिसाब बराबर करना	To bring a task to a finish
हिसाब बैठना	A favourable opportunity to present itself
हिसाब साफ करना (चुकाना)	To settle an account, To square accounts with
हींग लगे न फिटकरी	To achieve one's objective without efforts
हुक्का-पानी बंद करना	1. To boycott socially 2. To excommunicate 3. To freeze out 4. To ostracise
हुलिया तंग होना	To be in dire straits
हुलिया बताना	To describe the physical features of
हुलिया बिगाड़ना	1. To harass 2. To put into hot waters
हूक उठना	To feel the pangs of heart
हें-हें करना	To implore like a sycophant
हेकड़ी दिखाना	1. To be hubristic 2. To make a parade of one's vainglory 3. To show arrogance 4. To show false bravado
हेकड़ी भुला देना	To make one shed all one's vainglory
हेकड़ी भूल जाना	To shed one's arrogance and vainglory
हेय समझना	To make light of

होंठ काटना	To express helplessness
होंठ चबाना	To express resentment
होंठ फड़कना	To express intense emotional strain
होंठ बिचकाना	To show dislike
होंठ सी लेना	To keep mum
होनी होकर रहेगी	What is allotted, cannot be blotted
होम करते हाथ जलना	To suffer harm while doing something noble
होली जलाना	1. To destroy 2. To make a bonfire of
होश उड़ना/गुम होना	To be confounded To be in a blue funk To have the jitters
होश की बातें करना	To talk sense
होश ठिकाने आना	To learn a lesson
होश सँभालना	To come to age
हौसला तोड़ना	1. To demoralize the enemy 2. To lose heart
हौसला न पड़ना	To feel unequal to task
हौसला पस्त करना	To throw cold water on one's enthusiasm
हौसला बढ़ाना	To encourage
हौसला बाँधना	To summon up energies
हौसला रखना	To take heart
हौसला होना	To have the heart (to do)

लोकोक्तियाँ

अँखियाँ सुख, कलेजा ठंडा	Bright to sight, heart's delight
अंत भला सो भला	All is well that ends well
अंधविश्वास कमजोर व्यक्ति का धर्म है	Superstition is the religion of feeble mind
दाँत टूटा साँप जोर से फू-फू करता है	Shallow streams make much noise
अंधे अंधा ठेलिया दोनों कूप पड़ंत	When the blind lead the blind both shall fall into the ditch
अंधे के आगे रोए, अपने नैन खोए	Casting pearls before a swine
अंधे को खिलाना फिर घर छोड़कर आना	Dance and pay the piper too
अंधेर नगरी चौपट राजा	A confused ruler, a chaotic state
अंधों में काना राजा	A figure among cyphers
अंबा झोर चलै पुरवाई तब जानौ बरतवा ऋतु आई	If winter comes, can spring be far behind?
अकेला चना भाड़ नहीं फोड़ सकता	1. A lone soldier cannot win a war 2. One swallow does not make a summer

अक्ल बड़ी या भैंस	Knowledge predominates over mere strength
अक्लमंद को इशारा काफी	A nod to the wise
अग्र सोची सदा सुखी	Prevention is better than cure
अच्छों से भी गलती हो जाती है	The best cart may overthrow
अट्ट भी मेरी पट्ट भी मेरी	Heads I win and tails you lose
अति सर्वत्र वर्जयते	Excess of everything is bad
अधजल गगरी छलकत जाय	An empty vessel thunders much
अपना अपना पराया पराया	Blood is thicker than water
अपना तोसा अपना भरोसा	Everyone must stand on one's own legs
अपना नीगर पराया टींगर	The crow thinks her own birds fairest
अपना मकान कोट समान	Everyman's house is his castle
अपनी-अपनी ढपली, अपना-अपना राग	Let every herring hang by its own tail
अपनी इज्जत अपने हाथ	Respect yourself and you will be respected
अपनी गली में कुत्ता भी शेर होता है	Every cock fights best on his own dunghill
अपनी छाछ को भला कौन खट्टा कहता है	1. All his geese are swans 2. No one cries stinking fish
अपनी तकदीर आप बनती है	Every man is the architect of his own destiny
अपनी नाव खुद खेना	To paddle one's own canoe
अपनी लगाई आग में आप जल जाना	Hoist with one's own petard
अपने आपको अफलातून का नाती समझना	To grow too big for one's boots

अपने आपको लाट साहब का साला मानना	To have a swollen head
अपने दही को कोई खट्टा नहीं कहता	1. Every cook praises his own dish 2. Every potter praises his own pot
अपने पर पड़ जाए तो आदमी शेर हो जाता है	1. Man is a lion in his own cause 2. One fights best when driven to the wall
अपने मुँह मियाँ मिट्ठू	Self-praise is no recommendation
अब पछताए होत क्या जब चिड़ियाँ चुग गईं खेत	1. It is no use crying over the spilt milk 2. Lock the stable after the steed is stolen
अशरफियाँ लुटें, कोयलों पर मोहर	Penny wise, pound foolish
उल्टे बाँस बरेली को	1. Set the cart before the horse 2. Carrying coal to new castle
अहमद की पगड़ी महमूद के सिर	To rob Peter, to pay Paul

आ

आँख का अंधा नाम नयनसुख	To name a dunce Plato
आँख की ओट पहाड़ की ओट (आँख से ओझल, मन से बाहर)	Out of sight, out of mind
आँखों का लालच बहुत बड़ा होता है	Eye is bigger than belly
आए थे हरिभजन को ओटन लगे कपास	To set out for church, to strand in a lurch
आए सेर खाए सवा सेर	1. An angler eats more than he gets 2. Have a large mouth but a small girdle
आकाश से गिरा खजूर में अटका	Out of the frying pan into the fire
आगे की भैंस पानी पीए पीछे की पीए कीचड़	Bones for the late comers
आगे नाथ न पीछे पगहा	1. To have none to look after 2. Without any kith or kin
आधी छोड़ सारी को धावे, आधी मिले न सारी पावे	1. All covet, all lost 2. He who hunts two hares leaves one and loses the other

आधी बचै न कुत्ता खाए	To live from hand to mouth
आपकी बात सिर माथे	Your word is command to me
आपकी सीख आपको मुबारक	To keep breath to cool porridge
आपत्तिकाले मर्यादानास्ति	Necessity knows no law
आप मरे, जग प्रलय	After me, the deluge
आफत आई, दोस्त गए	1. Adversity flatters no man 2. When good cheers are lacking, friends will be packing
आ बैल मुझे मार	To stick one's chin out
आवाँ का आँवाँ ही खराब	Having a disgusting lot
आशा बड़ी मायावी होती है	He who lives in hope dances to an ill tune
आसमान का थूका मुँह पर पड़ता है	1. He who blows in the dust fills his own eyes 2. Piss not against the wind 3. Puff not against the wind
आहार-व्यवहार में लज्जा क्या	Fair exchange is no robbery

इंसान गलती करता है, भगवान माफ करता है	To err is human, To forgive divine
इतनी तारीफ कि वह शर्मिंदा अनुभव करे	To lay it on thick
इलाज से बचाव अच्छा	Prevention is better than cure
इश्क और मुश्क छिपे नहीं छिपते	Love and cough cannot be hidden
इसका क्या अचार डालोगे	Oh! the folly of keeping so much!

ईश्वर की माया कहीं धूप कहीं छाया	Change of fortune is the lot of life

उ

उँगली पकड़ते-पकड़ते पोंचा पकड़ लेना	Give a clown your finger and he will take your hand
उतने पाँव पसारिए, जितनी चादर होय	Cut your coat according to your cloth
उनका यहाँ से अन्न-जल उठ गया	The venue of his sustenance has shifted from here
उपदेश करने से स्वयं करना भला	Example is better than precept
उल्टा चोर कोतवाल को डाँटे	A thief threatening the constable
उल्टे बाँस बरेली को	To carry coals to Newcastle
उसका पाला अच्छे से पड़ा है	He has caught a Tartar
उसकी डाँट में तीखापन तो है किंतु घृणा नहीं	His bark is worse than his bite
उसके कीड़े पड़ें	May he suffer ruefully for his black deeds!

ऊ

ऊँची दूकान फीका पकवान	1. Great boast, little roast
	2. Great cry, little wool
	3. Much bruit, little fruit
ऊँट के मुँह में जीरा	1. A drop in the ocean
	2. Half a mouthful for a starving man
ऊँट मक्का को ही भागता है	Water finds its own level
ऊपर शहद भीतर जहर	The bait hides the hook
ऊपरी सज धज से कोई बड़ा नहीं बन जाता	If the beard were all, the goat might preach

ए

एक कान से सुनकर, दूसरे से उड़ा देना	Not to give patient hearing
एक चुप सौ को हराए	Silence is golden
एक जुर्म करे दूसरा भोगे	Ian commits the fault and May bears the blame
एक तिनके से हवा का रुख मालूम हो जाता है	Straws show which way the wind blows
एक तो करेला दूजे नीम चढ़ा	A pimple has grown upon an ulcer
एक-दो दिन मेहमान तीसरे दिन बला-ए-जान	To wear out one's welcome
एक बार खून मुँह में लगता है तो कभी नहीं छूटता	Once a whore, always a whore
एक फूल के खिलने से बहार नहीं आती	One swallow does not make a summer
एक मछली सारे तालाब को गंदा कर देती है	1. A black sheep infects the whole flock 2. One fish infects the whole water
एकहि साधे सब सधे सब साधे सब जाए	Rolling stone gathers no moss

एक ही थैली के चट्टे-बट्टे	Chips of the same block
ऐसी हँसी अच्छी नहीं जिससे दोस्ती में फर्क आए	Better lose a jest than a friend
ओखली में सिर दिया तो मूसलों का क्या डर?	1. He who would catch fish must not mind getting wet 2. Things once begun must be concluded at all costs
ओछे के पेट में बात नहीं पचती	Children and fools tell the truth
औरत का गुस्सा खुदा का कहर	Hell hath no fury like a woman scorned
औरन को गड्ढा चाहे ताको कूप तैयार	He who digs a pit for others himself falls into it

कंगाल का कोई क्या लूटेगा	The beggar may sing before the thief
कड़वे तथ्य को अच्छी भाषा में कहना चाहिए	Wrap up the bitter truth in clean linen
कड़ाही से उछला आग में गिरा	Out of frying pan into the fire
कथनी नहीं, करनी चाहिए	1. Deeds are fruits, words are but leaves 2. Saying is one thing, doing another
कफन में जेब नहीं होती	Our last garment is made without pocket
कभी इंसान कभी शैतान (दोहरी चाल)	Dr Jekyll and Mr Hyde
कर बुरा पा बुरा	Do evil and look for the like
कर भला हो भला	Light reflects light
कसूर करे कोई पकड़ा जाए कोई	1. Shoot at a pigeon and kill a crow 2. To bark up a wrong tree
कहने से कुम्हार गधे पर नहीं चढ़ता	Twenty can take a horse to water but none can make it drink

कहाँ राजा भोज कहाँ गंगू तेली	1. As different as chalk from cheese 2. Not fit even to hold a candle to
कहीं बूढ़े तोते भी पढ़ते हैं	1. An old dog learns no new tricks 2. Can you teach an old woman to dance?
कहे खेत की सुने खलिहान की कहे धान की सुने खलिहान की	To talk of chalk and hear of cheese
काक कहहिं पिक कंठ कठोरा	Kettle calls the pot black
काठ की हँडिया बार-बार नहीं चढ़ती	It is a silly fish that is caught with the same bait
कानी के ब्याह में नौ सौ जोखिम	There is many a slip between the cup and the lip
कानों सुनी बात आधी झूठी होती है	"They say so" is the half truth
काबुल में भी गधे होते हैं	There are black sheep in every society
काम का न काज का दुश्मन अनाज का	Not worth one's salt
काम, जीवन की जान	Business is the salt of life
काम बिसरा काम उसरा	Business neglected is business lost
किसी का व्यक्तित्व उसके खानदान से नहीं, गुण-दोष से जाना जाता है	Being born in a stable does not make man a horse
किसी को बैंगन बैरी, किसी को बैंगन पथ्य	1. One man's meat is another man's poison 2. What is sauce for the goose is not sauce for the gander

कीचड़ उछालते रहोगे तो दाग लगेगा ही	Throw dirt enough and some will stick
कुएँ का मेढक कुएँ के बारे में ही जानता है	The frog in the well knows nothing of great ocean
कुछ गुड़ ढीला कुछ बनिया	To have some deficiency at both ends
कुछ भी पहना दो, लंगूर लंगूर ही रहता है	An Ape is an ape, though clad in silk or scarlet.
कुत्ते भोखें हजार, हाथी चले बाजार	Dogs bark but the caravan goes on
कुत्ते की दुम बारह बरस गाड़ी टेढ़ी की टेढ़ी	Leopards never change their spots
कुत्ते को घी हजम नहीं होता	A low born person feels proud of his honour
कुत्ते भूँके तो चन्द्रमा को क्या?	Moon does not heed the barking dogs
कूड़े करकट के साथ काम की वस्तु फेंकना	To throw the baby with the bath water
कोई अंतर नहीं	Six of one and half a dozen of the other
कोठे वाला रोए, छप्पर वाला सोए	Uneasy lies the head that wears the crown
कोयले की दलाली में हाथ काले	Evil association must leave its impress
कोल्हू काटकर मुगदर बनाना	1. Cut down an oak and set up a strawdberry 2. Suffer a greater loss for smaller gain
कौए की चोंच में अंगूर	An Ass with two panniers
क्रोधी को चैन कहाँ	Angry man is seldom at ease

खरबूजे को देखकर खरबूजा रंग पकड़ता है	When the old cock crows the young cock learns
खरा खेल फर्रुखाबादी	Calling a spade a spade
खरी मजूरी चोखा काम	Fair day's work for a fair day's wage
खाओ तो ठेंगे से न खाओ तो ठेंगे से	Hobson's choice
खाली दिमाग शैतान का घर	1. An empty mind is a devil's workshop 2. An idle man's brain is a devil's workshop 3. Idleness is the rust of the mind
खाली बातों से पेट नहीं भरता	1. Belly has no ears 2. Fine words butter no parsnips
खाली बैठे उत्पात सूझे	Doing nothing is doing ill
खाली हाथ आए हो खाली हाथ जाओगे	Shrouds have no pockets
खिलाड़ी आसानी से दाँव में नहीं आता, पुराना	Old birds are not to be caught by chaff
खुला खेल	Something above board

ग

गंजों को कंघी अच्छी नहीं लगती	Scabby heads love not the comb
गधा धोने से घोड़ा नहीं होता गधा पीटने से घोड़ा नहीं होता	Crows are never the white for washing
गधी से गिरकर गुस्सा कुम्हार पर उतारना (गधे पर बस न चलना कुम्हारी के कान उमेठना)	To bark up a wrong tree
गधे को खिलाया न पाप न पुण्य	Kindness is lost on an ungrateful man
गरजी यार किसके, दम लगाई खिसके	A full purse never lacks friends
गरीब का सोना भी पीतल	Poor man's shilling is but a penny
गरीब की जोरू सबकी भाभी	A light purse is a great curse
गले पड़ा ढोल बजाना पड़ता है	What cannot be cured must be endured
गले पड़ी की खंझड़ी बजाने में ही खैर	1. Holding the baby, holding the bag 2. You must play on the drum hung from your neck

गले में माला, दिल में काला	Beads along the neck and the devil in the heart
गहराई में कमी होने से वक्ता विस्तार ज्यादा करता है	What the orators want in depth they give you in length
गाँठ का धेला, खातों के रुपयों से बड़ा (जैसा पैसा गाँठ का तैसा मीत न कोय)	A bird in hand is worth two in the bush
गाँठ में पैसा हो तो दोस्त घनेरे	In times of prosperity, friends will be plenty
गाँव बसा नहीं उचक्के आ बसे	Count not your chickens before they are hatched
गाय मारकर जूता दान	Steal a goose and give giblets in alms
गिरनेवाले मकान या डूबनेवाले जहाज को चूजे छोड़ देते हैं	Rats desert a falling house and a sinking ship
गुड़ की सी बात कहना गुड़ देने से अच्छा है	Honey in the mouth saves the purse
गुड़ न दे गुड़ जैसी बात तो करे	1. A good word costs nothing 2. There is nothing lost by civility
गुरुजी की मार बच्चे का संवार	Spare the rod and spoil the child
गुलामी की रोटी से मौत भली	It is better to die on your feet than to live on your knees
गेहूँ के साथ घुन भी पिस जाता है	When the buffaloes fight, crops suffer

घ

घर आते ही मुँह पर ताले	Hang up one's fiddle when one comes home
घर का जोगी जोगड़ा अन्य गाँव का सिद्ध	1. A prophet is seldom honoured in his own country 2. Familiarity breeds contempt 3. Distance lends enchantment to the view
घर की आधी भली, बाहर सारी नहीं	Dry bread at home is better than sweet meat abroad
घर की मुर्गी दाल बराबर	Too much familiarity breeds contempt
घर में नहीं दाने शादी चले रचाने	Love in a cottage
घर में दिया तो मस्जिद में दिया	Charity begins at home
घाटा मोटा, कागज छोटा	Difference is wide that the sheets will not decide
घायल की गति वैद्य क्या जाने	The wearer best knows where the shoe pinches
घूँघटवाली देख के भूल न जाना वीर	Beauty may have fair leaves yet bitter fruits
घोड़े को पानी दिखा सकते हैं किंतु पिला नहीं सकते	Twenty can take a horse to water but none can make it drink

चट मंगनी पट ब्याह	To implement a proposal without delay
चढ़े तवे पर रोटी सभी डाल लेते हैं	If a man ever falls all will bread on him
चमड़ी जाए पर दमड़ी न जाए (आदमी)	1. A close-fisted man 2. To be excessively stingy
चमड़े की पेटी कुत्ता रखवाला	To set the wolf to keep the sheep
चलता सिक्का खुशामद	The most current coin is flattery
चलती का नाम गाड़ी	Nothing succeeds like success
चाँद पर थूका मुँह पर आता है	He that blows in the dust fills his own eyes
चार दिन की चाँदनी फिर अंधेरी रात	A nine days' wonder
चिड़िया जान से गई राजा जी को स्वाद न आया	It may be death to one and not even fun to another
चित भी मेरी, पट भी मेरी	Heads I win and tails you lose
चुड़ैल भी सात घर छोड़ देती है	Wise fox will never rob his neighbour's henroost

चुल्लू-चुल्लू साधेगा तो द्वारे हाथी बाँधेगा	Take care of the pence and the pounds will take care of themselves
चूहों की मौत बिल्ली का खेल	It may be fun to you, but it is death to frogs
चोट्टी कुतिया जलेबियों की रखवाली	A fox should not be on the jury at a goose's trial
चोर के घर मोर	Catch a weasel asleep
चोर के घर छिछोर	Cuckold was very cunning
चोर की दाढ़ी में तिनका	A guilty conscience needs no accuser
चोर से कहे कि चोरी कर और शाह से कहे कि जागता रह	To hunt with the hounds and run with the hare
चोरी का माल कुछ धर्म खाते बाकी हलाल	Cheating the devil
चोरी करे मूँछों वाला, पकड़ा जाये दाढ़ी वाला	To bark up a wrong tree
चौबै जी गए छब्बे होने दूबे होकर लौटे	1. Camel going to seek horns, lost his ears 2. Go out for wool and come home shorn 3. Have tables turned on one

छठे कान में	To be likely to become public
छाज बोले सो बोले छलनी क्या बोले जामें छहत्तर छेद	1. Pot calling the kettle black 2. Person blames another for fault which he too has
छुद्र नदी भरि चलि उतराई	Little things are great to little men
छोटा मुँह बड़ी बात	Proud words from a weak stomach
छोड़े तो मरे, न छोड़े तो मरे (ऐसी स्थिति)	To hold wolf by the ears

जंगल में मोर नाचा किसने देखा	Wit in a poor man's breast is little thought of
जँह जँह चरण पड़े संतन के तँह तँह बंटाढार	It taints all it touches
जब अपनी उतरी तो दूसरे की उतारते क्या देर	Beware of him who regards not his reputation
उतर गई लोई तो क्या करेगा कोई	The shameless dread no society
जब जग नाचे नाच पेट पीठ के करने	Back and the belly keep everyone busy
जब जागो जभी सवेरा	It is never too late to learn
जब तक समुद्र रहेगा नमक तो मिलेगा ही	You never miss the water till the well runs dry
जर को जर ही खींचता है	Money begets money
जर, जोरू, जायदाद, झगड़े की जड़	Money, woman and land are the roots of all troubles
जल में मगर, थल में बोध	To be between Scylla and Charybdis
जहाँ मिले पाँच माली वहाँ बाग सदा खाली	Too many cooks spoil the broth
जहाँ सेर वहाँ सवा सेर	In for a penny in for a pound

जाए लाख रहे साख	1. Good name is better than bags of gold 2. Good name is better than a golden girdle
जाके पैर न फटी बिवाई, वो क्या जाने पीर पराई	Only the wearer knows where the shoe pinches
जाको राखे साइयाँ मार सके न कोय	1. Every bullet has its billet 2. Give a man luck and throw him into the sea 3. God tempers the wind to the shorn lamb
जाट जाटनी से पार न पावै बैल के चाबुक मारै	To bark up a wrong tree
जाट मरा तब जानिए तब तेरहवीं हो जाए	1. Do not say hello till you are out of the wood 2. Praise a fair day at night
जान लगी घटने खैरात लगी बटने	The chamber of sickness is the chapel of devotion
जाने किस का मुँह देखकर उठा है	To get out of bed on wrong side
जाने न सूझे कठौती से जूझे	A bad workman quarrels with his tools
जितना कष्ट उतना मेधावी	Genius has an infinite capacity for taking pains
जितना गुड़ डालोगे उतना मीठा होगा	If you pay peanuts you get monkeys
जितना फले उतना झुके	The boughs that bear the most, hang the lowest
जितना बड़ा पापी उतना बड़ा संत	The greater the sinner, the greater the saint

जितना मोटा आसामी उतना ही ज्यादा खतरा	Whiter the cow, the surer it is to go to the altar
जितने मुँह उतनी बातें	As many men, so many mouths
जिन खोजा तिन पाइयाँ गहरे पानी पैठ	1. Deeper the sweeter 2. The best fish swim near the bottom
जिनके दामन में दाग हों वे दूसरों पर कीचड़ न उछालें	Those who live in glass houses should not throw stones at others
जिम्मेदारी किसी और पर होना	Ball is in someone else s court
जिसका इलाज नहीं वह सहना पड़ता है	What cannot be cured must be endured
जिसका खाना उसका बजाना	He who pays the piper calls the tune
जिसका पल्ला भारी उसी से यारी	Coming down on the right side of the fence
जिसकी गोद में बैठना उसी की दाढ़ी नोचना	1. To bite the hands that feed one 2. To kick down ladder
जिसकी लाठी उसकी भैंस	Might is right
जिसे जोतना हो तो उसे भरपेट खिलाओ	Way to a man's heart is through his stomach
जिसने की शरम, उसके फूटे करम	Bashfulness is an enemy to poverty
जिसने चोंच दी वह चुग्गा भी देगा	God is the greatest provider
जिससे प्रेम होता है उसी के दुःख में आदमी परेशान होता है	Tongue always turns to the aching tooth
जीता वही जो अंत में जीते	He laughs best who laughs last
जैसा अन्न, वैसा मन्न (मन)	Men muse as they use

जैसा कच्चा माल, वैसा ही परिणाम	Garbage in, garbage out
जैसा देश वैसा भेष	While in Rome, do as Romans do
जैसा पैसा गाँठ का तैसा मीत न कोय	A pound in the purse is worth two in books
जैसा मालिक वैसा नौकर	Good jack makes a good jill
जैसा राजा वैसी प्रजा	Like master, like men
जैसी तेरी ढ़पली वैसे मेरे गीत	Work according to wages
जैसी बहे बयार पाट तब तैसी दीजै	Pull your hat on the wind's side
जैसे पाए वैसी पाटी	1. Like father, like son 2. Like tree, like fruit
जैसे साँपनाथ, वैसे नागनाथ	1. Difference is merely nominal 2. It is six of one and half-a-dozen of the other 3. Nothing to choose between
जो आया है सो जाएगा, राजा-रंक फकीर	Death follows birth, Death is sure
जो कुछ नहीं कर सकता वही उपदेश देता है	He who can, does; he who cannot, teaches
जो कमाए सो खाए	He who would eat the fruit must climb the tree
जो गरजते हैं सो बरसते नहीं	Barking dogs seldom bite
जो गलतियाँ नहीं करता वह कुछ नहीं कर पाता	Man who makes no mistakes does not usually make anything
जो चमकते हैं दमकते नहीं (सोना)	All that glitters is not gold
जो छूट गया सो छूट गया	Never mind what is left behind
जो जागत है, सो पावत है	It is the early bird that gets the worm

जो झुकना जानता है वह कभी नहीं गिरता	Reed before the wind lives on while mighty oaks do fall
जो ताको खाई खनै ताको कूप तैयार	They hurt themselves who wrong others
जो न देखे अगाड़ी, सदा रहे पिछाड़ी	Who looks not before finds himself behind
जो भूँकते हैं काटते नहीं	Great barkers are not biters
जो सुंदर होगा वह ईमानदार नहीं होगा	Beauty and honesty seldom agree

झगड़ालू कुत्तों की अयाल गंदी होती है	Quarrelsome dogs get dirty coats
झूठ के पैर कहाँ	A lie has no legs to stand upon
झूठ बहुत दूर तक नहीं चल पाता	Lies have short legs
झूठे दोस्त से खुला दुश्मन अच्छा	Better an open enemy than a false friend
झोंपड़ी में रहकर महलों के ख्वाब देखना	1. To live in a shanty and dream of plenty 2. To live on earth and dream of heaven

टके की बुढ़िया आना टांट मुड़ाई	1. Not worth powder and shot 2. Not worth the trouble
टाल-मटोल समय का चोर	Procrastination is the thief of time
टूट गई मंगनी रह गया ब्याह	Many a slip between the cup and the lip

ठगा बनिया, लुटा राजपूत किसी से नहीं बताते	A man's folly is his greatest secret
ठठेरे-ठठेरे बदलाई	Bargain between two equals
ठनठन गोपाल (ठनठन पाल मदन गोपाल)	1. A broken sack will hold no corn 2. Out of pocket
बड़ी खेती गामिनी गाय तब जानो जब मुँह में जाए	Many a slip between the cup and the lip
ठाले बैठे उत्पात सूझे	1. By doing nothing, we learn to do ill 2. Idleness is the rust of the mind

डाइन भी सात घर छोड़ देती है	A wise fox will never rob his neibhour's hen-roost
डूबते को तिनके का सहारा	A drowning man catches at a straw

ढाई ईंट की अपनी अलग मस्जिद	1. To blow one's own trumpet 2. To plough a lonely furrow
ढेर जोगी मठ उजाड़	Too many cooks spoils the broth
ढोंग वह सम्मान है जो दुर्गुण सद्गुण को देता है	Hypocricy is the homage which vice renders to virtue

तकदीर का लिखा मिटता नहीं	What is allotted cannot be blotted
तबेले की बला बंदर के सिर	The fault of the horse is put on the saddle
तराजू पर सोना सोना सब बराबर	The balance distinguishes not between gold and lead
तवा हाँडी को काला बताता है	1. The pot calls the kettle black 2. The sooty oven mocks the black chimney
तिल की ओट पहाड़	A mountain hidden behind a mole-hill
तू डाल-डाल मैं पात-पात	I can go deeper in the matter than you
तुरंत दान महाकल्याण	A stitch in time saves nine
तू मेरी डफली बजा, मैं तेरा राग अलापूँ	Claw me and I'll claw thee
तेते पाँव पसारिए जेती लंबी सौर	1. Cut your coat according to your cloth 2. To live within one's means
तेल देखो तेल की धार देखो	1. See which way the cat jumps

2. See which way the wind blows

तैराक ही प्रायः डूबते हैं	Good swimmers are often drowned

थोड़ा थोड़ा करके बड़े बड़े काम हो जाते हैं	Little strokes fell mighty oaks
थोड़ा बोलना सबसे अच्छा	Silence is golden
थोड़ी भी छूट बेजा फायदा	Give an inch and one would take an ell
थोथा चना बाजे घना	Empty vessels thunder much

दमड़ी की बुढ़िया टका सिर मुड़ाई	Game is not worth the candle
दम लगा घुटने खैरात लगी बटने	The devil sick would be a monk
दरिया में रहना और मगरमच्छ से बैर	It is hard to live in Rome and fight with the Pope
दाँत टूटा साँप जोर से फू-फू करता है	Shallow streams make much noise
दाड़ी में अक्ल नहीं होती	Brains don't lie in the beard
दादी को मत सिखलाओ कि जच्चगी कैसे होती है	Don't teach your grandmother to suck eggs
दान की बछिया के दाँत नहीं देखे जाते	1. Beggars and borrowers cannot be the choosers 2. Don't look a gift horse in the mouth
दान दिए ते न घटे धन, करती और लोभ	Alms giving never made any man poor
दाना न घास खरहरा छह छह बार	More praise than pudding
दाने दाने पर लिखा है खाने वाले का नाम	What is allotted cannot be blotted
दिल्ली की दरबारी से अपने गाँव की लम्बरदारी भली	Better be first in a village then second at Rome

दीन की सेवा ही दीनबंधु की सेवा है	Alms to the poor is lending to the lord
दीन को देना और दीनबंधु को देना बराबर है	Giving to the poor is lending to the Lord
दुधारू गाय की लात भी सहनी पड़ती है	1. If you enjoy the fire, you must put up with the smoke 2. Pain is forgotten when gain follows 3. Roses have thorns
दुनिया के सब काम, किसने किया तमाम	No living man can do all things
दुनिया में दूध का धुला कोई भी नहीं	He that is without sin among you let him cast the first stone
दुविधा में दोऊ गए माया मिली न राम	1. Between two stools, one falls to the ground 2. He who hunts two hares leaves one and loses the other
दुर्बलता में क्रोध अधिक	A little pot is soon hot
दूध का जला छाछ को फूँक-फूँक कर पीता है	1. A burnt child dreads the fire 2. Once bitten, twice shy
दूर के ढोल सुहावने	1. Distance lends enchantment to the eyes 2. Distant drums sound well 3. Grass is always greener on the other side of the fence
देखें ऊँट किस करवट बैठता है	Let us see which way the wind blows

देखे न अगाड़ी रहे पिछाड़ी	Who looks not before finds himself behind
देर आये दुरुस्त आये	Better late than never
दो का साथ, तीसरा आँखों में ठीकरा	Two is company, three is crowd
दो मुल्लाओं में मुर्गी हराम	Too many cooks spoil the broth

धन सबको अंधा कर देता है	Gold is the dust that blinds all eyes
धारा के आगे पुल नहीं बनता	It is ill striving against the stream
धीरा सो गंभीरा	Still waters run deep
धूल-धक्कड़ खाकर भी बढ़ना	To manage to live well despite abject poverty
धोबी का कुत्ता घर का न घाट का	Between two stools one cometh to the ground

न

नंगे का कोई क्या लेगा?	Beggar can never be bankrupt
नकल करना ही सच्ची खुशामद है	Imitation is the sincerest flattery
न नौ मन तेल होगा न राधा नाचेगी	If the sky falls we shall catch larks
न बासी बचे न कुत्ता खाए	To live from hand to mouth
न मिलने पर खराब ही सबसे अच्छा	Bad is the best
न रहेगा बाँस न बजेगी बांसुरी	No root, no fruit
न सुनोगे सीख तो मांगोगे भीख	Who would not be ruled by the rudder must be ruled by the rock
नाच न जाने आँगन टेढ़ा	1. A bad workman quarrels with his tools
नाचने लगे तो घूंघट गया	Poverty breeds contempt
नाम से हाजी वैसे पाजी	Carry two faces under one hood
नाली की ईंट कोठे चढ़ी (फिर भी गंध आती है)	Dogs bark as they are bred
नाव पानी में उतार दी आगे देखा जाएगा	Here goes, sink or swim

नीम हकीम खतराये जान	A little learning is a dangerous thing
नौ नकद न तेरह उधार	A bird in hand is worth two in the bush
नौ सौ चूहे खाए बिल्ली हज को चली	Singing all the days and going to church on Sundays

पक्के विरोधी दोस्त नहीं हो सकते	Parallel lines never meet
पछताए क्या होत जब चिड़ियाँ चुग गई खेत	1. It is no use crying over spilt milk 2. Mill cannot grind with water that is past
पट्ठों की जान गई पहलवान का दाँव ठहरा	The life of wolf is the death of the lamb
पत्थर घिसते-घिसते महादेव बन जाता है	1. He that travels far knows a lot 2. Practice makes a man perfect
परहेज इलाज से बेहतर है	Prevention is better than cure
पराया पराया, अपना अपना	Blood is thicker than water
पराए पूतों कौन सपूती	Put another man's child in your bosom and he will creep out of your elbow
पल में तोला पल में माशा	To blow hot and cold
पहले अपने, पीछे पराए	Blood is thicker than water
पाँसों का सबसे अच्छा फेंकना यही है कि उनको फेंक ही दें	The best throw with the dice is to throw them away

पाक दामन होना सबसे बड़ा हथियार है	Clear conscience is a sure card
पानी की कमाई पानी में गँवाई	Ill gotten, ill spent
पाप छिपाया पाप बढ़ाया	Dissembled sin is double wickedness
पास में न पैसा तो सुखचैन कैसा	Light purse is a great curse
पूत आपनो सब कहँ प्यारी	Every potter praises his own pot
पूत के पाँव पालने में दिखाई देते हैं	The child is the father of the man
पूरे न आसा करे उदासा	Hope deferred makes the heart sick
पेट-पीठ के कारने सब जग नाचे नाच	If it were not belly, the back might fear gold
पेट सब कुछ कराता है	The belly teaches all arts
पैठ आठवें दिन लगती है	Golden chances are but rare
पैसा गाँठ का, यार साथ का	Money in purse and the friend in need are the best companions indeed
पैसा तो प्यारा है पर चाम ज्यादा	The shirt is nearer than the coat
प्यादे से फरजी भयो, टेढ़ो-टेढ़ो जाए	1. Set a beggar on horse back and he will ride to the devil 2. Risen from the ranks must turn into cranks
प्रेम और खाँसी छिपते नहीं	Love and cough cannot be hidden

फजूलखर्ची पर कमर बंधी है	To burn the candles at both ends
फटी जेब में पैसा डालना बेकार	It is no use keeping money in a pocket that has a hole

बंदर की बला तबेले के सिर	Transference of the affliction to another head
बंदर क्या जाने अदरक का स्वाद	1. A blind man is no judge of colours 2. Caviar to the general 3. Do not cast pearls before a swine
बगल में छोरा नगर में ढिंढोरा	It's looking for a thing when it is in the mouth
बहुत ऊँचे आदर्श उन्नति में बाधक हो जाते हैं	The best is the enemy of the good
बच निकलना क्या कम बहादुरी है	Discretion is the better part of valour
बच्चा वही पहाड़ा बोलता है जो माँ सिखाती है	The child says nothing but what is heard by him
बच्चों और मूर्खों के पेट में बात नहीं पचती	Children and fools tell the truth
बजाज का बेटा कपड़े की भीख माँगे	Shoe-maker's son always goes barefoot
बड़े मियाँ तो बड़े मियाँ छोटे मियाँ सुहान अल्ला	The younger is even worse than the older

बड़े आदमी ही बड़े काम कर सकते हैं	Only an elephant can bear an elephant's load
बड़े बोल का सिर नीचा	Pride hath a fall
बड़े लाभ के लिए थोड़ी हानि	Venture a small fish to catch a great one
बड़ों के बड़े हाथ	Kings have long arms
बहती गंगा में हाथ धोना	To make hay white the sun shines
बाघ से लड़ने के लिए बघनखा	He must have iron nails that scratches a bear
बाप ने मारी मेंढकी बेटा तीरंदाज	Many talk of Robinhood who never shot with his bow
बारह बरस बाद घूरे के भी दिन फिरते हैं	1. Change is inevitable 2. Every dog has his day
बिना मरे स्वर्ग नहीं दीखता	1. He who would eat the nut must first crack the shell 2. The proof of the pudding is in the eating
बिना रोए माँ भी दूध नहीं देती	A closed mouth catches no flies
बिल्ली के सिरहाने दूध नहीं जमता	1. A watched pot never boils 2. Watching and anxiety won't hasten matters
बिल्ली (बार-बार का अपराधी) जल्दी नहीं मरती (बहुत सख्त जान)	Cat has nine lives
बीती ताहि बिसारि दे	1. Let bygones be bygones 2. To bury the hatchet
बुद्धिमान को इशारा काफी	A word to the wise
बुद्धिमान दूसरे की गलती देखकर अपने को ठीक कर लेते हैं	By other's faults wise men correct their own

बुभुक्षितं किं न करोति पापं	Hunger drives the wolf out of the wood
बुरी संगति से मनुष्य अकेला भला	Better alone than in bad company
बुरे को भगवान दूसरे का बुरा करने का साधन नहीं देता	Curst cows have short horns
बूँद-बूँद से घट भरता है।	Many a little, makes a mickle
बेवकूफों की कमी नहीं यारो एक ढूँढो हजार मिलते हैं	One fool is enough
बोया पेड़ बबूल का आम कहाँ से खाय?	1. Gather thistles and expect pickles 2. He that plants thorns must never expect to gather roses 3. Sow wind and reap whirlwind
बोलने से मौन भला	Speech is silver, but silence is golden

भ

भगवान और शैतान दोनों को एक साथ खुश नहीं कर सकते	You cannot have your cake and eat it
भगवान मुझे परिजनों से बचाए शत्रुओं से मैं अपनी रक्षा आप कर लूँगा	God, defend me from my friends, I will defend myself from my enemies
भगोड़ा सिपाही पलटन की बुराई करता है	Runaway monk never praises his convent
भय और प्रेम एक जगह नहीं रहते	Dread and affection never exist together
भीषण सिंधु तरंग में पहले पैठे कौन	Who should bell the cat
भूख में गूलर पकवान	Hunger is the best sauce
भूखा बहुत, आटा कम	Much bran, little meal
भूखे भजन न होय गोपाला	1. Empty sacks will never stand upright 2. Sharp stomach makes short devotion
भूत भला कहाँ लौटता है	Past cannot be recalled
भूसी बहुत आटा थोड़ा	Much bran, little meal
भेड़ की खाल में भेड़िया	Wolf in sheep's clothing
भैंस के आगे बीन बजाए भैंस खड़ी पदराए	To cast pearls before a swine

म

मखमल में टाट की बखिया	Round (square) peg in square (round) hole
मजबूरी का नाम महात्मा गांधी	To make a virtue out of necessity
मजे के लिए चाचा सलाह के लिए बाबा	If you wish for advice consult an old man
मझधार में नाव बदलनी ठीक नहीं	Never swap horses mid-stream
मतलबी यार किसके दम लगाया खिसके	Dinner over, away go the guests
मधुर वचन सौ क्रोध नसाही	A soft answer turns away wrath
मन चंगा तो कठौती में गंगा	To the pure, everything is pure
मनुष्य की पहचान उसकी संगत	A man is known by the company he keeps
मरे किसी को परेशान नहीं करते	The dead don't come for their defence
महंगा रोए एक बार सस्ता रोए बार-बार	A cheap buyer takes bad meat
महाभारत की पूरी तैयारी कर ली जाना	To be all set for action
माया बादल की छाया	Riches have wings
मार के आगे भूत नाचे	Spare the rod and spoil the child

मित्र वही जो विपत्ति में काम आये	A friend in need is a friend indeed
मीठा उत्तर टाले क्रोध	A soft answer turns away wrath
मीनमेख में पड़ने से असली बात रह जाती है	One cannot see the wood for the trees
मुँड़ी हुई भेड़ की तरह अमीर (कंगल-व्यंग्य)	As rich as a new shorn sheep
मुँह बंद कुत्ता क्या शिकार करेगा	Muffled cats catch no mice
मुँह में राम बगल में छुरी	1. Beads about the neck and devil in the heart 2. Honey tongue and heart of gall 3. Wolf in lamb's skin
मुफ्त की शराब काजी को भी हलाल	An open door will tempt even a saint
मुफ्त के बैल के दाँत क्या देखना	Never look a gift horse in the mouth
मूर्ख के तरकस में तीर नहीं टिकते	A fool's bolt is soon shot
मूर्खों के बीच मौन रह जाना अच्छा है	Where ignorance is bliss, it's folly to be wise
मूर्ख के लिए मौन भला	Cracked pipkins are discovered by their sound
मेह जो बरसे बैसाख, फूल खिले जेठ के पास	April showers bring forth May flowers
मैं भी रानी तू भी रानी कौन भरेगा घर का पानी	I stout and thou stout, who shall carry the dirt out
मौके की इंतजार में कुछ-न-कुछ करना	A bear sucking his paws
मौनम् सम्मति लक्षणम्	Silence is half-consent

मौत की कोई तारीख नहीं होती	Death keeps no calendar
म्याऊँ की ठौर कौन पकड़ेगा	1. Who will bell the cat 2. One taking the danger for a common cause

रक्षक भी, भक्षक भी	Run with the hare, hunt with the hounds
रसरी आवत जात तै सिल पै परत निशान	1. Constant dripping wears away a stone 2. Practice makes a man perfect
राजा पर भी नियम लागू होते हैं	Caesar is not above the grammarians
राजा भोज की पोशाक में गंगू तेली	Hog in armour
रात-दिन पिले रहना तेली का बैल बना देता है	Too much application makes one a drudge
राम राम जपना पराया माल अपना	A robber in the garb of a saint
रूप को अलंकार की आवश्यकता नहीं	1. A fair face needs no paints 2. Beauty needs no ornaments
रोग की जड़ खांसी झगड़े की जड़ हाँसी	Cough is the root-cause of all physical ailments and the jest of all conflicts
रोज के टपके से पत्थर भी घिस जाते हैं	Constant dripping wears away a stone
रोते हुए गए मरे की खबर लाए	1. A bird of ill-omen 2. Faint heart never won fair lady

लंबा टीका मधुर बानी दगाबाज की यही निशानी	Too much courtsey too much craft
लंबा पर सही रास्ता ही ठीक	Farthest way about is the nearest way home
लकड़ी के बल बंदर नाचे	Need makes the old wife trot
लाल बुझक्कड़ बूझिया, और न बूझा कोय	The ass waggeth his ears
लालच में आया और डूबा	One who falls into temptation, comes to grief
लैला की खूबसूरती देखनी हो तो मजनूं की निगाह से	Beauty lies in the eyes of the beholder
लोभी का पेट सदा खाली	A greedy man is always a needy man

वक्त पर एक टाँका नौ का काम देता है	A stitch in time saves nine
वक्त बड़े-से-बड़े घाव भर देता है	Time is the best healer
वह लड्डू जो मिला नहीं सबसे मीठा	Forbidden fruit is sweet
विवशता का नाम कर्त्तव्य-परायणता है	To make a virtue of necessity
वीरता का काम न चाहे नाम	Good deeds need no show
वीर भोग्या वसुंधरा	Fortune favours the brave
वो दिन गए जब खलीलखां फाख्ता उड़ाया करते थे	Gone is the goose that was golden

शक्करखोरे को ईश्वर शक्कर देता है	Spend and God will send
शक्ल चुड़ैल की मिजाज परियों का	Fine feathers make fine birds
शब्दों से आदमी की पहचान होती है	Fool is recognised by a spoken word
शेख क्या जाने साबुन का भाव	A blind man is no judge of colours
शेर और बकरी एक घाट पर पानी पीते हैं	Equitable justice is meted out to all, high and low
शेर की खाल में गधा	An ass in lion's skin
शेर चूहों का शिकार नहीं करते	The eagle does not hawk at flies
शेर भैंसे को मारेगा खरगोश को नहीं	The brave fight with persons worth their steel

संकल्प सफलता की कुंजी है	Strong will is the key to success
संशयात्मा विनश्यति	Success eludes the doubting Thomas
सत डिगा जहान डिगा	When character is lost all is lost
सत्ता के बागी ही सत्ता परिवर्तन में क्रांतिकारी भूमिका निभाते हैं	It is invariably the insurgents who become revolutionaries
सब दिन होत न एक समान	He who laughs on Friday will weep on Sunday
सबसे बड़ा नंग नंग से बड़ा परमेश्वर	Beware of him who regards not his own reputation
सभी अपना-अपना स्वार्थ देखते हैं	Every miller draws water to his own mill
समझ के खर्चे समझ के बोले	Keep your purse and your mouth close
समय पर टाँका नौ का काम देता है (समय पर लगाए एक टाँके से बहुत बचत होती है)	A stitch in time saves nine
समरथ को नहिं दोष गुसाईं	1. King does no wrong 2. Rich men have no faults

समाई के बाद मश्क भी फूट जाती है	It is the last straw that breaks the camel's back
समुद्र और श्मशान किसी को इंकार नहीं करते	Sea and the gallows refuse none
समुद्र पर पुल बाँधना	To set the Thames on fire
सम्मान के योग्य वही होते हैं जिनको उसकी कोई आवश्यकता नहीं होती	Those who deserve a monument do not need it
सस्ता रोए बार-बार, महँगा रोए एक बार	1. Best is best though costly 2. Cheap goods are dear in the long run 3. The cheap buyer takes bad meat
सस्ता सौदा, ज्यादा लाभ	Light gains make a heavy purse
सहज पके सो मीठा होय	Slow and steady wins the race
सांच को आंच नहीं	Pure gold does not fear the flame
साँप का काटा रस्सी से डरे	A burnt child dreads the fire
साँप के सँपोले ही होंगे	As the crow is, so the egg shall be
साँप छछूंदर की-सी गति	To be on the horns of a dilemma
साँप निकल जाने के बाद लकीर पीटना	To kiss the hare's foot
साझे की खेती गूजर खाएँ	Everybody's business is nobody's business
साझे की हाँडी चौराहे पर फूटे	1. Responsibility of all is responsibility of none 2. A common horse is worst shod
साधु के भेस (वेष) में डकैत	To sail under false colours

सिखैया नाऊ का काटेगा बटाऊ का	Barber learns to shave by shaving fools
सिर्फ बातों से काम नहीं चलता	Bare words buy no barley
सुंदर चेहरों का न मन मैला	A fair face cannot have a crabbed heart
सुख में सभी साथी होते हैं दुःख में कोई नहीं	Laugh and the world laughs with you, weep and you weep alone
सुधार में देर क्या सबेर क्या (सुबह का भूला शाम को घर आ जाये तो भूला नहीं कहलाता)	It is never too late to mend
सूखे पेड़ पर कोई नहीं बैठता	1. No bird rests on a dry lone tree 2. None befriends the poor
सूत न कपास जुलाहे से लट्ठम-लट्ठा	1. Counting one's chickens before they are hatched 2. To sell the skin before you have caught the bear
सूरत से सीरत का अंदाज नहीं होता	1. All that glitters is not gold 2. Beauty is but skin deep 3. Don't go by appearance
सेवा बिना मेवा नहीं	He who would eat the kernel must crack the nut
सोते नाग को मत जगाओ	1. Let sleeping dogs lie 2. Not to wake up the sleeping dog
सोना और पीतल जैसा	As like as chalk to cheese
स्वर्ग की गुलामी से नरक का राज भला	1. Better be the head of an ass than the tail of a horse 2. It is better to rule in hell than to serve in heaven

हथेली पर सरसों नहीं जमती	Rome was not built in a day
हमाम में सब नंगे	All cats look grey in the dark
हमारी बिल्ली और हमीं से म्याऊँ	Frankstein's monster
हर सीपी से मोती नहीं मिलता	You cannot make a mercury of every log
हर मर्ज की दवा	Heal-all, panacea
हराम की कमाई धर्मखाते में लगाई	To steal a goose and give giblets in alms
हराम की कमाई हराम में गँवाई	1. Easy come, easy go 2. Ebb will fetch off what the tide brings in
हरि अनंत हरिकथा अनंता	Infinite is the Lord and infinite are His glories
हल्दीघाटी की गति	To meet Waterloo
हाथ कंगन को आरसी क्या	1. A self evident fact requires no proof 2. Seeing is believing 3. The proof of the pudding is in the eating

हाथ में माला दिल में काला	Cross on the breast and the devil in the heart
हाथ में माला दिल में भाला	A fair face and foul heart
हाथ सुमरनी पेट कतरनी	Counting the beads and concealing a dagger in the breast
हाथी के दाँत खाने के और दिखाने के और	All that glitters is not gold
होई है सोई जो राम रचि राखा	Man proposes, God disposes
होनहार बिरवान के होत चीकने पात	Coming events cast their shadows before
होनी थी सो हो गई, सीख करे अब क्या	When a thing is done advice comes too late